GLOBAL PLAN FOR EMPLOYMENT

GLOBAL PLAN FOR EMPLOYMENT

A NEW MARSHALL PLAN

ANGELOS TH. ANGELOPOULOS

PRAEGER SPECIAL STUDIES • PRAEGER SCIENTIFIC

Library of Congress Cataloging in Publication Data

Angelopoulos, Angelos Theodōrou, 1904–
  A global plan for employment.

  Includes index.
  1. Economic policy. 2. International economic
relations. I. Title.
HD82.A6345 1983   337   83-10987
ISBN 0-03-063798-8
ISBN 0-03-063847-X (pbk.)

Published in 1983 by Praeger Publishers
CBS Educational and Professional Publishing
a Division of CBS Inc.
521 Fifth Avenue, New York, New York 10175 U.S.A.

© 1983 by Praeger Publishers

3456789 052 987654321

Printed in the United States of America
on acid-free paper

Professor Angelopoulos' diagnosis of the present economic ills of the world makes sense to me. I find it refreshing to have the views of an academician who has the experience of international banking, the close presence of the developing world leaders on the problems of stagflation, global debt, and possible lines of recovery. There is a captivating youthfulness and freshness in his ideas on these subjects.

Professor Angelopoulos sees clearly the dangers inherent in the present economic impasse of the world, especially in the confrontation between the developed industrial nations and the emerging developing nations. The debt situation of the latter group is truly explosive. During 1982, the world economy was taken to the brink of an abyss. Luckily, restrictive policies were reversed at the last minute, but those actions did not solve the problem; they merely prevented a massive collapse that could have generated a breakdown of the present economic system on the order of the 1929 collapse.

The concept of Global Keynesianism introduced in this book is very attractive, coming at a time when national Keynesianism is being challenged by proponents of theories who led the world economy down the road to the near collapse during the summer of 1982. There are many analytical and technical deficiencies of crude monetarism and crude supply-side economics, not to mention rational expectations, on both the theoretical and applied sides of our subject. These deficiencies are being exposed by the unfortunate turn of events and by the ongoing debates in individual countries, especially in academic circles, but the boldness of Professor Angelopoulos' vision to extend the Keynesian principles to a total world scale leapfrogs the defenses and provides us with beautiful offensive concepts. He is perceptive in noting how the successes in applying the Keynesian medicine of the past 30 years can be parlayed into another generation of high performance for the world economy beyond the turn of the century. This is the hope that is inspired by his concept of Global Keynesianism.

But for the practical problems of the day, Professor Angelopoulos has an attractive policy prescription that needs no elaborate analytical theory; it rests simply on his good common sense. Unless a bold new scheme is introduced beyond the day-by-day mending of the cracks in the international debt structure, we run the danger of losing the whole show. His plan, detailed in this book, for handling the interest and amortization burdens of the debt incurred by the developing countries ranks with the Marshall Plan that was so successful in restoring the alliance of the industrial democracies after World War II. The Marshall Plan will probably be rated by historians as one of the greatest economic achievements of the 20th century. We need a similar vision now to treat the oppressive burden of debt that has been incurred by the developing countries, and Professor Angelopoulos' Plan should rank at the head of the list of proposals that are now being considered. It offers an orderly way around the impasse. It is steeped in economic justice and equity, and if it is not given proper attention by people who fear losses, the outcome may well be that these same interests will suffer much more disastrous losses.

From the home of the classics, we have a viewpoint that serves well in the modern debate, perhaps reflecting the discipline of classical training and reasoning.

Lawrence R. Klein

ACKNOWLEDGMENTS

I should like to express my sincere thanks to Professor Lawrence R. Klein who had the kindness to read the entire manuscript, to give me valuable and constructive comments, and to write the Foreword to this book. I am very grateful to him.

I should also like to express my thanks to Professor Hourmouzis G. Georgiadis of the OECD and to Dr. Melvin Fagen, former Senior Advisor to the Executive Secretary of the United Nations Economic Commission for Europe.

I discussed with each of them several aspects of the manuscript and I profited from their insightful reactions. Professor Georgiadis in particular was a valuable contributor of ideas at critical junctures of my own thinking.

The editors of Praeger Publishers significantly improved the manuscript with their suggestions and initiatives.

CONTENTS

Table

Figure

THE IMMENSE PROGRESS OF SCIENCE AND TECHNOLOGY REALIZES THE DREAM OF ARISTOTLE

If the nineteenth century was the age of Great Britain and Europe, if the twentieth century is that of the United States and the Soviet Union, the twenty-first century is likely to be the age of the Third World: Asia, Africa, and South America.

Is this a prediction of an impending revolution that is destined to influence the whole future of mankind? If we are really to understand the great problems of today, to reveal their causes, and to foresee their effects on the economic and social structure of the world of tomorrow, we must wake up to the fact that we are living in a new period of history. A period in which economic, social, political, and cultural conditions bear little resemblance to those that have prevailed up to now. Science and technology are accelerating the course of social and economic development at an unprecedented rate. Indeed, the development process is directly determined by the pace of advances in science and technology.

To the extent that science "masters" nature, so man can perform a given amount of work in greater or less time. Machines, today, cannot only substitute for muscular effort, but also for human brainpower. Does not the fact that cybernetics, computers, and robots with electronic "brains" are replacing men in many fields, assert that the dream of *Aristotle* has now become a reality? In the fourth century B.C., Aristotle wrote:

If every instrument could, on an order received, or even intelligently anticipated, work of its own accord, like the statues of Daedalus, or the tripods of Haephestus which betook themselves unaided to the conclaves of the gods, if shuttles could weave alone, if the plectrum itself could play the zither, then employers would be able to do without workers, and masters without slaves.[1]

Today, the truth of this ancient vision is confirmed.

The study of humanity's evolution through the centuries shows that it is marked by a continuous succession of economic, social, and political transformations. Parallel with these changes, there is a periodic readjustment of the State's objectives, in order to bring them into line with new economic and social conditions, as well as a transformation of the social conscience and of man's attitude towards life.

Science and Technology
Determine Economic Evolution

Technology plays a part in every sphere of human activity and its progress throughout history has to a great extent determined the course of economic and social development.

Each phase of the mechanical age has left its imprint on civilization. The industrial revolution of the eighteenth century, based on the invention of the steam engine, put an end to feudalism, transformed production methods, manners of thought, and the style of living, and brought the capitalist system into being. The second industrial revolution, which began about 1880, was primarily due to the generalization of the use of electricity: it created large-scale enterprises, led to the rationalization of industry, and carried capitalism to its zenith. For nearly two centuries, the world has lived under an expanding capitalist system. The State has repeatedly had to modify its objectives, and with every change a new social equilibrium has been established. These changes have always been followed by a growth in production and an improvement in the standard of living.

It was also technical progress that made it possible for certain countries to attain their economic power. Great Britain achieved supremacy by being the first to intensively exploit the technical inventions of the second half of the eighteenth century. With a certain time lag, France and Germany followed Great Britain's example. Electricity and oil opened up new possibilities for industry and have enabled the United States to become the dominant economic power during the twentieth century. After the first and the second world wars, the Soviet Union accelerated its progress and became, with the United States, a major power. This brought about changes in international economic balance of power.

The constant process of transformation has now become more rapid than ever before. Methods of production, means of transport and communications, political and social institutions, ideas and systems are evolving at an unprecedented pace. The immense advances in science and technology — thanks to recent discoveries made especially in the fields of nuclear energy,[2] space research, cybernetics, and information techniques — are likely to accelerate the rhythm of social progress at a rate hitherto unknown. This progress is also likely to overturn existing economic, social, and political structures and, finally, to lead society toward a sociopolitical system unified on a worldwide scale.

The fact that we have been able to leave our planet and go to the moon and return, the fact that today it is possible to explore space by teleguided means, indicates that science and technology have placed at our disposal powerful instruments for opening up or even creating great perspectives for the future of mankind.

The technological revolution has brought about a profound modification in the structure and balance of the economies and will lead to a new way of life, characterized by a progressive reduction of the time devoted to labor and an increase in the time available for leisure. This social restructuralization is, in fact, a primary necessity in limiting the unemployment that is likely otherwise to take on alarming dimensions in the years to come.

OTHER FACTORS THAT ACCELERATE
THE ONGOING TECHNOLOGICAL REVOLUTION

Some other factors, which appeared principally after the Second World War, constitute active and powerful forces destined to accelerate the technological revolution. The most important of these factors are:

1. *The Division of The World into Two Blocs*. The world today contains within it a contradiction. The division in two opposing blocs is both an obstacle to the prosperity of mankind and a danger for peace, but at the same time it has the effect of accelerating scientific and technological progress.

Who can deny that the technical-scientific revolution of our epoch has been the result of military motivation, or that this has hastened its development? If the world were not divided, atomic energy and telematics, electronics, and other scientific advances would not have been so rapidly integrated into industrial production and the exploration of space and travel to the moon would not yet have taken place.

Because of the exacerbating military competition between the West, the East, and China, this division has led to antagonistic efforts to develop new armaments. Deep ruptures and radical value changes are taking place within international society in this multipolar world. The fact that cracks are appearing within each of the two blocs complicates the situation and tends to overturn traditional international relationships.

2. *The Entry of Third World Countries onto the International Scene*. There are now more than 100 Third World states, and they already exercise important political power in the United Nations organization. Because of their efforts to catch up with the industrialized countries, their demographic explosion and their immense material and human potential, these countries are likely to play a leading role in the world and eventually to overturn the traditional equilibrium of international society. Robert Oppenheimer, the great man of science, declared shortly before his death: "When the myriad

populations which now live on the edge of starvation and misery awake to their situation and to ours, . . . I fear what can result."

I must, at this point, emphasize my conviction that the economic and social development of the Third World countries is not only a condition for the prosperity of the developed countries but has become, inevitably, a fact. The countries that are now poor will succeed in overcoming their backwardness in a shorter period of time than was necessary for the countries that are at present developed. The industrialization of the young nations will sooner or later be realized under new and unique conditions, even if the rich countries reduce or eliminate their assistance. This will take place because of the progress of technology and the internal contradictions in the industrial countries. The only result of a negative attitude on the part of the rich countries will be the creation of a hostile climate that will inevitably lead to bloody conflicts. The powerful human masses of the Third World, which will represent three-fourths of humanity at the end of this century, will be able, especially through the instruments provided to them by science and technology, to change the geopolitical map of the world.

3. *The Pressure of the Workers and of Youth.* Workers organized in trade unions, and young people, students, and intellectuals are continuing their pressure to obtain a more equitable distribution of the fruits of collective progress. This reinforces the trend toward a more just and humane society. Their claims go beyond more immediate material objectives. They challenge the very structure of society, both capitalist and communist; their questioning of social organization reflects a profound discontent.

This trend, particularly of youth, toward a more active participation in economic and political life, toward a more rational and equitable administration of the resources of all countries, toward a permanent improvement in the quality of life, will, with time, become stronger and have an ever-increasing influence.

No one can ignore the importance and significance of these powerful forces. The people of the twentieth century think differently from those of the nineteenth century. Confronted with the hard realities of our times, people refuse to accept the "present social order" as inevitable and unchangeable. They believe, on the contrary, that it must and can be reoriented. They are not content just with having won their political rights, but intend to use them to secure their economic and social rights as well. They demand a greater measure of social justice, a larger and more equitably distributed national income, and a higher standard of living. They no longer regard poverty and inequality as "natural" conditions but they do regard "the right to the pursuit of happiness" as natural. They believe that full employment, social security, and the adequate remuneration of labor, with an income sufficient to cover the essential needs for themselves and their families, together with full respect of their individual liberties and human rights, are not simply the duties but the obligations of government. And, moreover, they are convinced that all essential preconditions of progress and development come within the framework of the government's responsibilities.

The people of today are seeking a better world, a more just, a more humane one, not only on a national level but also on the worldwide scale.

To achieve such a target, a permanent readjustment to these requirements of governments' objectives and policies is urgently needed together with efforts to coordinate national policies to lead to such an international goal. In the absence of such national priorities and international objectives, a chain of global reinforcing recessions becomes inevitable and with them social regression and despair.

In my book, *The Third World and the Rich Countries*, first published in 1972,[3] I emphasized that an international economic recession would become inevitable if appropriate measures were not implemented without delay. It was at that very time that I foresaw the necessity for, and formulated the general outline of, a scheme for *a new worldwide Marshall Plan* in order to avoid the inevitable economic crisis. The crisis period 1974-82 confirmed this prediction in a striking way.

In the present book, following an analysis of the international economic situation and its repercussions, a plan is developed in a cohesive and concrete way for a global solution to the current economic impasse.

A journey I made recently to China and India has led me to the conclusion that the plan proposed here would be an effective solution to the world stagnation — stagnation that has hit the industrial countries with particular force. Taking into account the enormous needs of the developing countries — for capital equipment and services — and the surplus production capacity and unemployment resulting from nonutilization of a large part of the productive apparatus by the industrial countries, one may ask why such a plan, useful and necessary both for the industrial and the poor countries, has not been developed. The application of such a plan is a matter of great urgency.

The author would be happy if the thesis put forward in this book caused responsible statesmen to liberate themselves from old outmoded doctrines and to pursue a new international development strategy capable of enabling the world economy to overcome the present impasse. For, as J. M. Keynes said, "It is not sufficient to understand new ideas but it is necessary to escape from the old ones which extended their ramifications to all the corners of our minds."

NOTES

1. Aristotle *Politika*, A^4 (1253^{b33}-1254^{a1}).
2. The economic, social, and political aspects of the atomic era are examined in a book that I published following the First International Atomic Conference, held in Geneva. This book, published first in French (librairie Générale de Droit, Paris, 1955), has been translated into English, German, Italian, Spanish, Russian, Japanese, and Greek. The English edition bears the title: *Will the*

Atom Unite the World? Economic, Social and Political Aspects of the Atomic Age (London: Bodley Head, 1957).

    3. English edition by Praeger Publishers (New York, 1972).

GLOBAL PLAN FOR EMPLOYMENT

1

AN ECONOMIC CRISIS OF
ALARMING DIMENSIONS

CONTINUED STAGNATION
OF ECONOMIC GROWTH

Everywhere today the basic causes of the crisis that since 1974 has shaken the world economy, and more particularly the economy of the industrial countries, are of great concern.

The enormous increase in unemployment, particularly high inflation, chronic deficits in balances of payments, soaring interest levels, perverse fluctuations in currents of exchange rates, insufficient investments, steep drops in prices of raw materials, costly energy resources, the continued decline of economic growth — these are characteristics of an entrenched crisis that is gradually becoming deeper and more universal. It is not exclusively a crisis of capitalist countries but of socialist countries as well. In fact, we are faced with a crisis of our civilization, since political unrest, civil wars, acts of anarchy and terrorism, and other signs of upheaval emanate from the economic crisis and create, particularly among industrial countries, a general anxiety concerning the world of tomorrow.

The present economic situation is especially disturbing because, despite the hopes that arose as a result of the application of measures and mechanisms of adjustment undertaken by various governments, the recession steadily becomes worse.

An Unfounded Forecast

The transition from a state of relative prosperity, which prevailed during the 1960s, to a sudden state of crisis was a shock for all the industrial countries in the Western camp. These countries believed that economic progress would continue generally undisturbed or at least that their economies would always be under control. Even the International Development Strategy, adopted on October 24, 1970 by the General Assembly of the United Nations, foresaw for the 1970-80 period an average rate of growth of 6 percent annually for all countries combined. The Western industrial world thus was hardly aware of the fact that the beginning of the recession, with all its tensions and repercussions, was near. Indeed, in 1973, on the eve of the oil crisis, though the economic situation showed signs of a beginning weakness, the governments directly concerned still envisaged the future with confidence.

Undoubtedly, one of the most striking developments, which coincided with the beginning of the "stagflation" process was the increase in the price of crude oil. This price, after a long period of stability, more than quadrupled in 1974 and increased again by 150 percent between 1978 and 1980.

Nevertheless, it should be recognized that such increases in oil prices by the OPEC countries were not the only cause of economic disorder. They reinforced the influence of several other factors that had already begun to provoke important disturbances in the functioning of the world economy, and they had the effect of revealing an overall weakness of the economic system. It may even be suggested that if the rise in oil prices had not led to the slow-down that the world economy has been experiencing since 1974, the structural imbalance of the international economic system alone would undoubtedly have provoked a serious economic crisis in the early 1980s at the latest.

This continuous divergence between forecast and reality should have, at the very least, alerted the forecasters to the possibility that they were using parameters of an already obsolete economic era to forecast a newly emerging economic structure. Forecasting, however, became a self-justifying technique instead of an objective tool. While abundant evidence that a profound structural change in the international economy had occurred was gathering, the forecasters continued undisturbed in their narrow calculations, based on continuation of existing economic and social structures.

In spite of the extent and intensity of the economic instability that has emerged, the attention given by Western governments to these factors was insufficient to lead them to adopt a new strategy capable of dealing with the problems posed over the short and long term. Repeated international "summit conferences" were held, as were successive meetings between representatives of all industrial countries, but no appreciable progress toward the adoption of a new strategy was made.

This failure of governments to address the growing and chronic unemployment issue, to undertake a collective action aimed at identifying the true reasons for the crisis, and to adopt remedial measures, explains in part the weakness of their forecasts of economic activity, which have been at best risky. These forecasts have been based on hypotheses that were increasingly irrelevant and on goals that were increasingly contradictory.

Thus, in January 1976 the Organization for Economic Cooperation and Development (OECD) drew up projections of the growth of total production in certain industrial countries, but these projections, which proved to be nearly twice as high as the actual results

TABLE 1.1
Increase of Total Production
(annual average changes)

Country	Forecast 1975-80	Actual 1970-80		Actual 1980-82
United States	6.25	3.6	2.9	1.7
Federal Republic of Germany	4.50	3.6	2.8	−1.0
France	5.75	3.3	3.6	0.7

Source: OECD, *Economic Outlook* (various issues).

obtained in the period 1975-80, were soon shown to be unreal, as shown in Table 1.1.

Reduction of Growth Rates

The average annual growth rate in the industrial countries fell to 3.1 percent during the decade of the 1970s, as compared with 5 percent in the previous decade.[1] In spite of some improvements, especially in the years 1977-78, the situation has greatly deteriorated since 1979 (see Figure 1.1). According to international organizations, the average growth in Gross National Product (GNP) in the industrial countries as a group amounted to only about 1 percent for the year 1980. The same growth rate is estimated for the period 1981-83. The growth rate of the big industrial countries of the OECD for the period 1981-83 is shown in Table 1.2.

The situation in the developing countries, although appreciably better in percentage terms at the beginning of the 1970s, has shown since 1976 a rapid slowing down of growth rates. These rates differ in various groups of developing countries. The situation is particularly alarming in the non-oil-producing developing countries as a whole and especially in the poorest of the developing countries.

Table 1.3 shows the evolution of the growth of GNP in the 1960s and the 1970s in totals and per capita. It may be seen from this that the growth rate in the industrial countries dropped from 5 percent to 3.1 percent during the 1970s, while the rate in the developing countries remained at about the same level, dropping only from 5.6 percent to 5.3 percent. On the other hand, the GNP per capita in the developing countries declined from 5.3 percent to 2.9 percent. For the poorest developing countries, this decline is even more accentuated − from 4 percent to 1.7 percent − mainly because of the greater increase of population.

The slowdown in growth rates has also affected the socialist countries. Following the relatively high growth rates of the 1950s and the 1960s, there has been a notable reduction during recent years in the growth rates of the Eastern countries forming the Council of Mutual Economic Assistance (CMEA) group. According to a study of the Economic Commission for Europe, the net material

FIGURE 1.1
GNP Growth
(Percent change for 24 OECD countries)

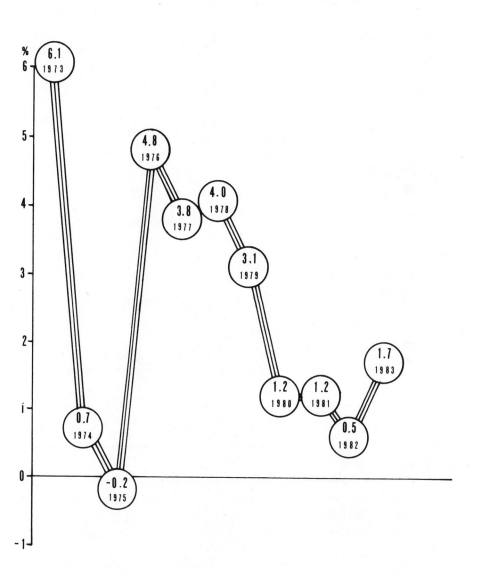

TABLE 1.2
GNP Growth Rate for the Years 1981, 1982, 1983

Countries	1981 share of the total OECD GNP	Average 1970-80	1981	1982	1983*
United States	38.5	2.9	1.9	−1.7	2.0
Japan	14.8	4.8	3.0	2.5	3.5
Germany	9.0	2.8	−0.2	−1.25	−0.5
France	7.5	3.6	0.3	1.5	1.0
United Kingdom	6.5	1.9	−2.2	0.5	1.0
Italy	4.6	3.1	−0.2	0.7	0.25
Canada	3.6	4.1	2.9	−5.0	1.25
Total of the above countries	84.4	3.2	1.3	−0.5	1.7
Other countries of the OECD	15.6	3.1	0.7	0.5	0.7
Total of OECD	100.0	3.2	1.2	−0.5	1.5

*Estimate.
Source: OECD, *Economic Outlook* (Paris, December 1982).

TABLE 1.3
Growth of GNP and GNP per capita, 1960-80
(Average annual percentage growth rates. At 1977 prices)

	GNP		GNP per capita	
	1960-70	1970-80	1960-70	1970-80
All developing countries	5.6	5.3	3.1	2.9
Low income countries	4.2	4.0	1.8	1.7
Middle-income countries	6.0	5.6	3.5	3.1
Industrial countries	5.0	3.1	3.9	2.4
Socialist countries	n.a.	5.2	−	3.8

Source: World Bank Annual Report, 1980, p. 16.

FIGURE 1.2
Industrial Countries, Output and Prices
(percent changes from preceding year)

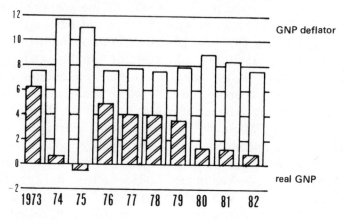

Source: IMF Survey, June 1982.

product (NMP) of all the countries of Eastern Europe and the USSR has increased only by 2.4 percent in 1979 and by 1.2 percent in 1981, as contrasted with the average of 5.2 percent for the 1970s. There has also been an increase in inflation rates. Apart from the reduction in real production in all the industrial countries of the West and East, there has also been an important drop in productivity, due particularly to a failure to renew industrial equipment and to the use of obsolete technologies; the drop is also attributable to the maintenance in employment of surplus or underutilized manpower for social reasons.

Deterioration in Payments Deficits

Besides unemployment and inflation, which will be examined in the following chapter, a further consequence of the economic crisis has been the deterioration of balances of payments, reflected in the large amounts of foreign exchange distributed in an unequal manner. This situation is the result of a deep modification of the structure of international trade. The volume of monetary transfers arising from the increase in oil prices has, in particular, brought about the formation of large surpluses in the current accounts of the oil-producing countries and considerable deficits in the oil-importing countries. Table 1.4 shows the changes in the world balances on current accounts between 1973 and 1980 by groups of countries.

Monetary stability is a function of economic stability and monetary instability is the result of turbulent economic conditions. In the post-1973 economic world, which has been marked by chronic and expanding balance-of-payments deficits, by long-lasting and unyielding inflation, by low growth and stagnation, by increasing numbers of unemployed, monetary policy has had an increasingly destabilizing effect. As national governments found themselves, one after the other, locked in high-budget deficits, in large part the consequence of low growth, sluggish aggregate demand, and lack of flexibility in their ability to cut expenditures, including military and unemployment benefits, they were forced to make monetary policy the economic instrument for realizing their economic objectives. As may be seen from Table 1.4, the countries most affected are the developing countries that do not export oil. Their balances have been continuously in deficit throughout this period; the deficit reached $99 billion in 1981 with a likely trend toward further increase in the coming years. On the other hand, the industrial countries, as a result of a recycling of petrodollars, reestablished a virtual equilibrium in their external payments, with a sizable surplus of $30.5 billion in 1978. However, the new increases in oil prices in 1978 and 1979 have reversed the situation and have brought about deficits of $10 billion in 1979, $44 billion in 1980, but only $3.0 billion in 1981. Clearly, the oil-exporting countries are the great beneficiaries of the increases in oil prices. Their surplus of $68 billion in 1974 fell to only $3 billion in 1978 as a result of the volume of their imports. As a result of the latest price increases, a record surplus of $116 billion was recorded by these countries in 1980 and of $69 billion in 1981.

In fact, it is the oil price increases that have played an important role in the deterioration of the external payments balances on current accounts. In the event that the oil-exporting countries proceed with their economic development as they have in the past, this might prove less unfavorable for industrial countries.[2] As things stand at the moment, however, this appears unlikely.

TABLE 1.4
Balances on Current Accounts, 1973-82
(in billions of dollars)

	1973	1974	1978	1980	1981	1982
Industrial countries of which:	18.0	−14.0	34.0	−40.0	− 1.0	6
7 industrial countries	12.7	− 4.9	33.9	−17.5	16.0	19
Other industrial countries	5.0	− 8.9	− 3.5	−26.2	−14.0	−11
Developing countries:						
Oil-exporting countries	7.0	68.0	3.0	116.0	69.0	15
Non-oil-exporting countries	−12.0	−37.0	−39.0	−86.0	−101.0	−91

Source: IMF Annual Report, 1982, p. 18, and other issues of IMF.

Monetary Disorder

Following the abandonment of the Bretton Woods System —
which had been until that time the fundamental base of the international monetary system — fixed exchange rates were replaced by
floating rates that reflect both the effects of inflation and the business-cycle conditions in each country. The situation became compli-
cated following continuous increases in interest rates — which
proved a serious obstacle to economic activity. For let us not forget
that monetary policy is economic policy. Without a prosperous and
stable economy, the maintenance of monetary stability becomes
impossible.

This does not mean that the role of monetary policy in a period
of recession is secondary. Monetary policy can act upon inflation,
on expenditures, on the balance of payments, and on savings. But
this can only take place if it is applied on the basis of a well-estab-
lished plan that has as its objective a reinforcement of economic
activity within the framework of an appropriate structural reform.
When restrictive monetary and budgetary measures are not made part
of a coherent and coordinated plan for the whole economy, they
tend not to encourage but rather to harm economic activity and
in certain cases even to accelerate recessionist tendencies. This has
been the experience during the 1974-80 period.[3]

That is why, for example, all the proposals of the Executive
Council of the IMF and of the Committee of Twenty on the need for
a reform of the monetary system, for a process of adjustment, or for
a better management of global liquidities, have until now remained
ineffective. Thus, even a cursory examination of the characteristics
of the present economic crisis clearly shows its structural nature,
its profound depth and its disturbing dimensions.

GRIM PROSPECTS FOR THE COMING DECADES

If present economic policies continue, prospects appear gloomy
for the next two decades until the year 2000. In fact, the World Development Report published by the World Bank, paints a pessimistic

picture of the prospects for world economic growth in the next five or ten years and this is repeated in the 1982 report.[4] The World Bank analysis, which bases its projections on a high-growth hypothesis as well as on a low-growth hypothesis, indicates that there are disquieting signs that the latter hypothesis rather than the former is likely to prevail. In this case, the growth of GNP per capita on average will be about 1 percent for the period 1980-90. This forecast was arrived at by many other, as well as more recent, projections.

The projections made by other international organizations, such as the United Nations Conference on Trade and Development (UNCTAD), OECD, Wharton, The European Economic Commission, and other institutions all forecast disappointing prospects for tomorrow's economy.[5]

Evolution of Economic Indicators

Based on the present state of the world economy and on existing projections we could outline the expected evolution of the principal economic and social indicators during the coming decades to the year 2000 as follows:

• *Economic growth of industrial countries until the year 2000 will be appreciably inferior compared with the preceding decades.* The annual rate is expected to be around 2 percent as against 5 percent in the 1950s and 1960s. According to the UNCTAD study, a return to the former rates is "unlikely in the foreseeable future." The annual growth rates for the world economy in the coming decades as projected by UNCTAD are shown in Table 1.5.

Among industrial countries, Japan is likely to come out of the recession in a stronger position; it would probably continue to develop at a growth rate almost double that of other industrial countries. With a low unemployment level (only 2 percent of its active population against 10 percent in other industrial countries), an ever-increasing productivity (5 percent compared to 1.5 percent), insignificant military expenditures compared to other industrial countries, and expanding commercial relations particularly with Asian countries, Japan will dominate the international market in the coming decades at the expense of other industrial countries.

TABLE 1.5
Average Annual Rates
(percentages)

	1960-70	1970-80	1980-90	1990-2000
Industrial countries with				
market economy	5.0	3.2	2.4	2.2
Japan*	(10.8)	(5.2)	(4.0)	(4.0)
Socialist countries of				
Eastern Europe	6.6	5.3	3.5	3.5
Developing countries	5.9	5.6	4.2	7.0
Socialist countries of				
Asia (China)	6.8	5.5	5.0	7.0

*Japan's figures appear in parentheses because it is only one of the industrial countries with a market economy.

Source: UNCTAD, Report on Commerce and Development, 1981, pp. 91 and 140.

However the forecasts of UNCTAD seem to be optimistic. According to the last OECD Economic Outlook, for the first three years of the 1980s the average growth rate of the big European countries is estimated to be 0.7 percent, for the United States, 1 percent, and for Japan 3 percent.[6] For this reason it is not certain that — if there is no change in economic policy — the forecast rate of 2.4 percent for the decade 1980-90 will be reached. According to forecasts made by Wharton, the growth prospects of the eastern socialist countries are no more than 2.5 percent for the period of the 1980s in contrast to the more optimistic estimates by UNCTAD.

In developing countries, despite their present difficulties, the growth rate will be higher, almost double, compared to that of industrial countries. During the years 1981-82, for example, when the growth rate in the industrial countries was only 1.5 percent, in the Asian countries the average growth rate was 7 to 8 percent.[7]

The justification of this forecast is partly based on the fact that during the period 1975-82 the developing countries registered a remarkable performance in investment, which amounted to, and frequently exceeded, 25 percent of GNP. At the same time, industrial countries, by giving preference to consumption over investment, brought about a continuous decline in their capital formation. This rapid development will create pressure on the rest of the world. The expansion of commercial relations between South and South will constitute another unfavorable factor for the trade of industrial countries.[8]

Even though the road followed by socialist countries is sharply different from that followed by industrial countries of the West, these countries registered an impressive growth between 1950 and 1979. But it appears that their growth in the years to come will be slower and lower than that of the preceding decades. UNCTAD forecasts for socialist countries of Eastern Europe show an average growth rate of 3.5 percent for the 1980s and 1990s, against approximately 7 percent in the 1960s and 1970s.[9] For China, on the contrary, the growth rate is estimated around 7 percent.[10]

• *Unemployment will increase.* The industrial countries of the West, except Japan, are threatened with having 50 million unemployed before the year 2000, or more than twice today's figure. Unemployment benefit payments will lead to permanently increasing budgetary deficits.[11]

• *Inflation persists and will continue to do so at high rates.* Under present conditions, there are no signs of a reversal of inflationary tendencies. In the United States and the United Kingdom the reduction in inflation has hitherto been realized at the expense of higher unemployment levels.

• *Monetary disorder will also be aggravated in coming years and a financial crash is to be feared in case the problem of overindebtedness is not reasonably solved in a timely fashion.* This crash would upset the foundations of the international financial and monetary system. High-interest rates, which are the result of an imbalance between the supply of and demand for capital in the international market, and which are being reinforced by national monetary policies in key industrial countries, will continue to be a serious obstacle to a recovery of international economic activity. Actually the interest rates have fallen, but it is not certain that this situation will be maintained for a long period.[12]

• *Regarding the energy problem, there is, for the time being (1983), a provisional slackening of demand and a consequent fall in oil prices.* Despite this, however, oil expenditures will continue to exert pressure on deficits, particularly for developing countries. In

the event that the OPEC countries can no longer dispose of important surpluses, the outcome will be a decrease in their imports and
a consequent fall in economic activity in the industrial countries.

•   *Finally, the gap between countries of the North and South will*
continue to widen due to population growth that will impinge
adversely on GNP per capita and, despite a relative improvement in
overall economic performance, poverty will continue to be wide-
spread.

Thus prospects for the international economy and particularly
those of industrial countries are very gloomy, if present policies
are continued. The presence of a constantly increasing army of
unemployed will lead to social and political instability that will
constitute a grave menace to social peace in all countries of the world
and also to world peace. Moreover productivity will tend to decline.
As Professor Paul W. McCracken recently stated, "By the latter part
of the last decade (i.e., 1975-80) on the average for the major industrial economies, gains in productivity were so lethargic that 65 years
would be required to achieve a doubling of material levels of living,
compared with a pace in the 1960s that would double real incomes
every 16 years."[1][3]

Indeed the dynamism of the world economy has been at a
"virtual standstill" during the last ten years. Speaking before the
United Nations General Assembly, the president of the World Bank,
Mr. A. W. Clausen, underlined the consequences of this situation:
"If just 5 percent of the world's productive capacity now stands idle
because of the recession – and that is probably a conservative
estimate – each year's lost production is about of the same order
of magnitude as the *total* income of the poorer half of humanity.[1][4]
The result of this evolution is, as Professor Xenophon Zolotas
observed in a recent study, that the economic growth observed in
the period of the 1960s and 1970s has been accompanied by a
decline in social welfare.[1][5]

ANXIETY AND RECOMMENDATIONS,
BUT NO ACTION

It is not only the present situation of the world economy that
should attract the attention of responsible political leaders, but even

more the gloomy prospects for the future. The application of a new policy is an imperative necessity.

M. Gaston Thorn, president of the European Community Commission, in a speech to the European Parliament on February 16, 1982, warned member countries that "the Community is in danger and could collapse if it does not solve its economic problems."

What are governments doing in the face of this situation? What are the policies recommended by the various international organizations such as the United Nations, OECD, the World Bank, and the IMF responsible for worldwide economic strategies?

These institutions in general give absolute priority to the fight against inflation and recommend as the means, the adoption of monetary and budgetary measures that restrict global demand.

Is inflation truly the principal cause of the present stagflation or is it merely the symptom? Certainly the existence of inflation aggravates the economic situation. However, inflation is not merely a monetary phenomenon; it is above all an economic one. For it is the outcome of imbalance between global supply and global demand caused by insufficient productive investments that further aggravate the insufficient global demand (consumption plus investments). This is where the principal cause of the crisis lies.

Furthermore, this fight against inflation through restrictive monetary and budgetary measures limits economic growth and increases unemployment, which has taken on disquieting proportions.

Does the reduction in the rate of inflation eliminate unemployment and strengthen economic growth? The Federal Republic of Germany, with a low rate of inflation amounting to only 5.3 percent, experienced an increase in unemployment of 43 percent in a single year (1981), bringing the total number of unemployed to more than 2 million by the end of 1982. In addition, the maintenance of a low rate of inflation in that country has not succeeded in accelerating its growth, which between 1981-83 has had an average growth rate of −0.3 percent.

In the United Kingdom, Mrs. Thatcher's government brought down the inflation rate from 18 percent in 1980 to 6.6 percent in 1983. But at what price? By a 103 percent increase in the number of unemployed, who in March 1983 numbered 3.2 million and an average growth rate between 1981 and 1983 of zero percent. Is that the mission of the state in the twenty-first century?

Will the Folly of the 1930s be Repeated?

In fact, the method of combating inflation conceived and recommended as top priority by international organizations only leads to a vicious circle or an impasse that brings about negative effects on the economy without opening the way to any valid solutions either in the short or long term. We find ourselves, therefore, almost in the same situation as in the beginning of the 1930s. At that time, the effects of the great crisis of 1929 continued to be very serious. There was a large reduction in production, a high rate of inflation, a wave of strikes with acute social conflict and vast unemployment in the industrial countries, especially in the United States, France, Germany, and the United Kingdom.

Now, at the beginning of the decade of the 1980s, the questions must be asked, do we find ourselves confronted with the very same situation as existed in the 1930s? Is it not true, that now and again we see the same symptoms of a deep and generalized crisis afflicting the world economy?

The leaders of our countries have been meeting every year since 1970 in an effort to find appropriate means of combating inflation, but without success. They have postponed putting into operation radical measures to cope with the problems of our times. Their attitudes at present are similar to those of the prewar leaders. At that time too, economic conferences were held that did not lead to effective solutions. Toward the middle of 1933, at a time of full crisis, when 30 million workers were unemployed in the industrial countries, an economic and monetary conference was held in London to deal with this grave situation. After 36 days of discussions, this conference reached the conclusion that a solution to the economic problem was impossible. "After very long exchanges of views," we read in their final communiqué, "it was agreed that solutions on the international level to these fundamental problems were for the moment impossible to formulate and *that it was preferable under these conditions to adjourn the discussion.*"[16]

The same mentality exists today. In fact, during the numerous Summit meetings held in recent years, apart from diagnostic statements on the actual economic situation, no policies have been adopted that can lead the economies of the world out of the present crisis.[17]

The situation prevailing today is the same as on the eve of the Second World War. At that time, governments also tried in vain to resolve economic problems in accordance with the dogmas of the classical school that gave priority to monetary and budgetary measures, leaving the other economic measures aside. But as the British economist J. M. Keynes demonstrated, priority belongs to economic growth and social well-being. Monetary policy is only one of the many policy instruments and not a policy target in itself. And as we know, it was the application of Keynesian principles that maintained industrial countries for a quarter of a century in the position, not only of being able to provide full employment for their own population, but of being able to absorb 2 million immigrants into their labor force as well.

Today, as on the eve of the Second World War, there is once more a divorce between relevant theory and reality. Once more an attempt is being made to solve the current economic problems with outdated theories applicable to an earlier but now past economic structure. No wonder that economic variables such as productivity, economic growth, and money no longer behave according to traditional economic doctrines. A new economic order cannot be created by adhering to old principles that have proved totally ineffective and by ignoring the radical economic changes of our times that have made inevitable and mandatory a new policy for the economy and society. As Professor E. Carr, the historian, remarked, the survival of theories that have been bypassed by events has always had a disastrous influence on economic life and leads to chaos, to social disorder, and finally to war.[18]

It took the shock of the Second World War with all of its destruction to bring an end to the classic economic era. It was only after that war that a deep change was made in the economic policies applied, a change that under the inspiration of the Keynesian theory allowed the Western world to experience, for a quarter of a century, a great degree of sustained economic and social progress.

Today, the same historical law requires radical changes in the outmoded economic policies now in place. This need is urgent if we are to avoid disaster.

INDUSTRIAL COUNTRIES FACE
A DOUBLE CHALLENGE

In the face of this critical situation, the industrial countries, which with 28 percent of the world's population produce 80 percent of world income, must accept a double challenge: on the one hand, to move the world economy out of its present impasse and establish a new order that would assure a prosperous and continued development; and on the other hand, to end the poverty and misery that reign in the greater part of the world and constitute a danger for peace.

In order to meet this double challenge, the industrial countries must resolve four great problems that at present prevent the revival of the world economy. These problems are:

1. Unemployment, which has taken on alarming dimensions.

2. The tremendous increase in military expenditures, particularly those of the two superpowers.

3. The overindebtedness of developing countries, the annual servicing of whose loans overburdens the budgets of those countries and prevents their development.

4. The energy crisis, which continues to create chronic deficits in all non-oil-producing countries and developing countries, and which impedes their economic and social progress.

If solutions to these problems, analyzed in the following chapters, are not found, not only will economic revival become impossible, but the present crisis will become deeper with grave repercussions for all mankind.

NOTES

1. The statistical data referred to in this study are taken from the most recent publications of the International Monetary Fund (IMF), the International Bank for Reconstruction and Development (IBRD), and the Organization for Economic Cooperation and Development (OECD), particularly the annual

reports of the IMF and the IBRD for 1982 and various publications of the OECD issued in 1980-82. Also, the *Wharton World Economic Review*, various issues.

2. The effects of the increase of the oil prices are examined in Chapter 5: "The Energy Crisis and the Problem of Oil."

3. The repercussions of the monetary policy on the world economy are examined according to the LINK system in a study prepared by Laurence Klein, Richard Simes, and Pascal Voisin, published in August 1981 under the title "Coordinated Monetary Policy and the World Economy," (Philadelphia: LINK CENTRAL, University of Pennsylvania).

4. World Bank, *World Development Report*, 1980, p. 113, and subsequent issues.

5. See in particular, World Bank, *World Development Report*, 1980. Washington, D.C. See also: UNCTAD, *Report on Commerce and Development, 1981* (New York: : United Nations, 1982); OECD: *Face au Future* (Paris 1979); European Commission, *Programme á Moyen Terme* July 1981; Ralph Dahrendorf, *La Crise en Europe* (collective work) (Paris: Fayard, 1982); United Nations, *The Future of the World Economy* (New York, 1977); Wharton, *World Economic Outlook*, December 1981 and subsequent issues; Alfred Sauvy, *Mondes an Marche* (Paris: Calmann-Levy, 1982); United Nations, *International Development Strategy for the Third United Nations Development Decade* (New York, December 1981). Also: Vassily Leontief, *The Future of the World Economy* (New York: United Nations, 1976); Economic Impact: *New perspectives on development*, no. 4 (studies by numerous authors) (Washington, D.C., 1982); Raymond Barre, *UNE Politigue Pour l'avenir* (Paris: Piou, 1981); Wharton, *The World Economy at a Crossroads, International Financial Crunch, Crisis or Crunch?* Special Report, (Philadelphia: March, 1983); H. G. Georgiadis, L. R. Klein, V. Su, *International Coordination of Economic Policies*, in "Greek Economic Review," Vol. 1, No. 1, August 1979; C. Fred Bergsten and Lawrence R. Klein, *The Need for Global Strategy*, "The Economist", 23 April 1983; Peter F. Drucker, The Age of Discontinuing, New York: Harper Colophone Books, 1978; Wharton, *Centrally Planned Economies Outlook*, various issues (Philadelphia); Wharton, *Foreign Exchange Outlook*, various issues (Philadelphia).

6. OECD, *Economic Outlook*, 1982.

7. The average growth rate, in percent, for this period in the following countries was:

Singapore	7.5
Thailand	6.5
Indonesia	7.4
Malaysia	6.2
Philippines	4.0

8. According to OECD, the portion of exports from developing countries to oil-importing countries has risen from 18.5 percent in 1970 to 20.8 percent

in 1977. Exports of these same countries to OPEC countries went up from 4.8 percent to 9.1 percent. *The OECD Observer*, January 1982, p. 8.

9. UNCTAD, *Report on Commerce and Development*, p. 170.

10. According to the Economic Plan Commission of China, the target for the year 2000 is to increase four times the industrial and agricultural production of the year 1980. That means an annual average of 7.2 percent ("Beijing Information," October 4, 1982). According to the same review, the annual average of this production between 1980-81 was 9.2 percent.

11. The problem of unemployment is examined in the following chapter.

12. The problem of interest rates is examined in Chapter 4.

13. Paper delivered at the Conference on Economic Policies in the U.S., Sept. 10, 1981, Paris, France, p. 3.

14. Second Committee, November 12, 1982.

15. Xen Zolotas, *Economic Growth and Declining Social Welfare* (New York: New York University Press, 1982); see also, OECD, *L'Etat Protecteur en Crise* (Paris, 1980).

16. See "L'Etat et la Prospérité Sociale" (Paris: Pichon et Durand-Auzias, 1949), p. 27.

17. Characteristically, in a recent article on this point the *Economist* wrote: "The world economy is edging its way on to the ground that has lain fallow for 50 years. The parallels with the 1930s are not close enough to justify all the gloom of those years, but they do serve as a warning of the risks that lie ahead. So far, politicians have shown little understanding of what those risks look like in the early 1980s. They are still relying too much on the common-sense rules developed in the 1970s, the first three of which are now being broken." (*Economist*, May 8, 1982, p. 16). The *Washington Post* has also recently commented on the reemergence of Herbert Hoover's policies on the U.S. economic issue: "The analogy between Hoover's years and the present situation is exceedingly inexact" (*International Herald Tribune*, August 9, 1982).

18. E. Carr, *The Conditions of Peace* (London, 1942).

2

CAUSES AND CONSEQUENCES OF UNEMPLOYMENT

THE ALARMING INCREASE IN UNEMPLOYMENT

Unemployment has been growing at a high rate for the past decade and is assuming ever more disturbing proportions. The number of unemployed in the industrial countries of the West is now approaching 30 million. This represents almost 10 percent of the total active population. Even more threatening is the steep rise in the number of unemployed in recent years. Between 1979 and 1981, the rate of unemployment in the European Community countries increased by 55 percent and between 1981 and 1983 by 32 percent. In the United States between 1979 and mid-1983 the unemployment rate increased almost by 75 percent.[1] Thus, since 1979, the number of jobless seeking work has continued to grow without interruption.

Table 2.1 shows the proportions of the unemployed to the total active population in selected countries.

Two countries lead the unemployment ratio list: the United Kingdom with 13.5 percent of the active population and Canada with 12.3 percent.

I acknowledge the contributions of Professor H. G. Georgiadis, particularly in technical aspects concerning the effects of technology on employment.

TABLE 2.1
Unemployment in the Active Population

	1960-69 (average)	1970-80 (average)	1981	1983*
Percentages of Unemployed				
United States	4.6	6.1	7.5	10.2
Japan	1.3	1.7	2.25	2.21
Fed. Rep. Germany	0.8	2.4	5.0	8.5
U.K.	2.0	4.7	10.5	13.5
Italy	5.1	6.3	8.25	9.8
France	1.5	4.0	7.5	9.7
Belgium	–	–	11.6	12.0
Canada	–	–	7.6	12.3
TOTAL OECD	–	–	7.0	9.3
Numbers of Unemployed (in Millions)				
OECD Europe	–	–	13.9	18.4
North America	–	–	9.2	12.9
TOTAL OECD	–	–	24.8	33.3

*Estimate.
Source: OECD, *Economic Outlook*, 1982, 1983.

Certain branches of economic activity are more affected by unemployment than others. According to European Community data, between 1976 and 1981 the textile industry lost 8.8 million jobs, footwear and clothing 9.1 million, metallurgy 8.3 million, and automobiles and shipbuilding 6.3 million. This confirms the fact that in addition to the unfavorable effects of an internal recession, the European Community, which represents a vast market, has also become particularly vulnerable, in the competitiveness of some of its industries, to the assaults of the newly industrialized countries. The European Community forecasts that unemployment will continue to grow, at least until 1985, though perhaps at a slower pace.

Labor Absorptive Capacity
in Europe, Japan, and the United States

Unemployment as a problem appears more significant for the economies of Europe than for the economy of either the United States or Japan. The capacity of the European economies to create new jobs is much more limited than those of North America or Japan.

During the 1970s, the active population of the United States increased from 83 million in 1970 to 103 million by the end of the decade, or by 20 million. Some 17 million of these became gainfully employed. In contrast, during the same period, the active population of the four main European countries, which was 92 million, increased by 4 million, but of this increase only 1 million became gainfully employed. The above comparisons show that, during the entire last decade, for every ten newcomers on the job market in the United States and in the four main European countries, about nine found jobs in the United States compared to only three in the European countries.[2] In the case of Japan, where there was an increase in the active population of 4.5 million, 4 million became gainfully employed, which explains why in that country, unemployment has never exceeded 2.25 percent during the last decade.

These comparisons show that labor absorption and active employment policies remain much more of a critical problem for the governments in Europe than for those of the United States and Japan where the dynamism of the economic systems tends to lessen their impact.

UNEMPLOYMENT OF YOUNG PEOPLE

One of the most frightening facets of the employment crisis is its effect on young people in particular. In the industrial countries, almost 50 percent of the unemployed are in the 15-25 age group.

The problem of youth unemployment has been reexamined recently by the International Labor Organization (ILO). According to the *Report of the Director General*, "One inhabitant out of five

FIGURE 2.1
Standardized Unemployment Rates

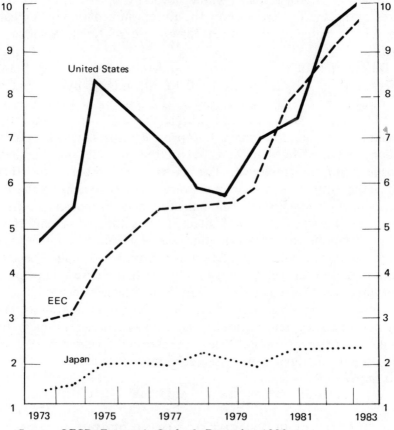

Source: OECD, *Economic Outlook*, December 1982.

FIGURE 2.2
Total Employment
(1973 = 100)

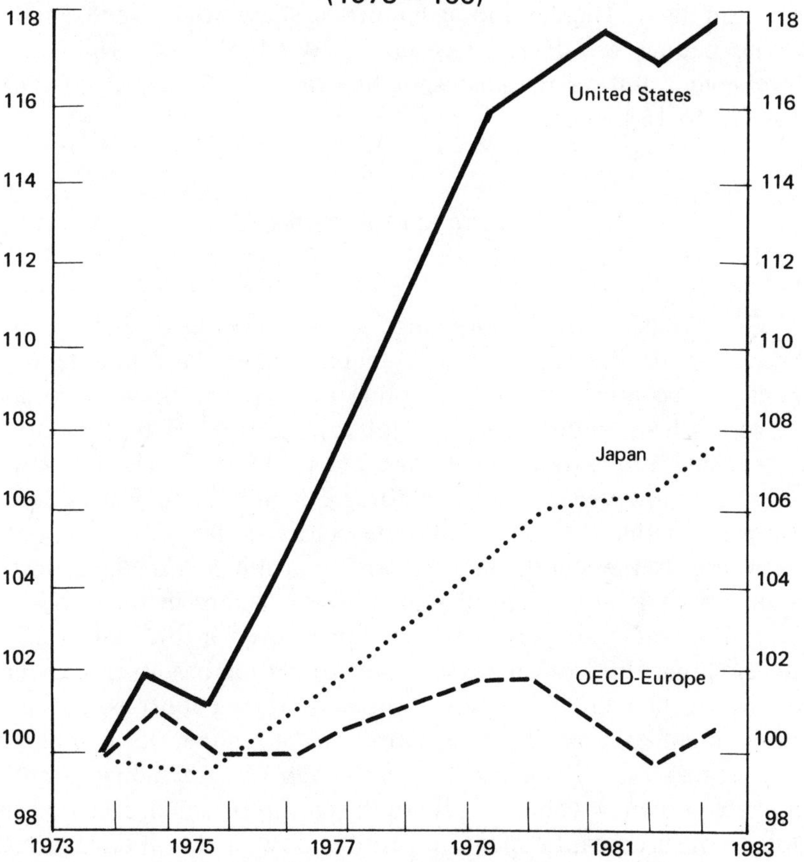

Source: OECD, *Economic Outlook*, December 1982.

in the world today is between 15 and 24 years of age. Over three-quarters of them, or 665 million, are concentrated in the developing regions, with 60 percent living in Asia."[3]

Projections for the year 2000 show an even greater concentration of youth in the developing countries. As Table 2.2 shows, by the year 2000, the number of young people will have surpassed the 1 billion mark. The developing countries' share of almost 900 million young people will increase from 77 to 84 percent, while in the developed countries the corresponding figure will drop significantly, from 23 to 16 percent.

Access to Employment

But, what are the employment prospects of these young people? According to the ILO report, "unemployment and underemployment are so prevalent among young people that there is hardly a country where finding a decent job and getting off to a good start in working life is not something of a problem."[4] The number of young unemployed stood in 1980 at 6.5 million in Europe alone, compared with a total of 1 million ten years earlier.

Acute as the youth unemployment problem is in the industrial countries, it is a problem of immense dimensions in the developing countries, where, according to the report, even in the case of adults "at least one third of the male active population has no employment worthy of the name." In many of the developing countries, youth unemployment exceeds 50 percent of the total number of unemployed, approaching even 70 percent in some countries, including populous India, as shown in Table 2.3. It can thus be pretty much accepted that global youth unemployment constitutes now, and will remain in the foreseeable future, one of the highest-ranking problems of our time.

This tremendous problem is of serious concern to governments, for the difficulties that the young encounter in entering active economic life are not only of a business-cycle nature; they are mainly of a structural nature and in order to deal with them, new short- and long-term policies are needed to open new employment opportunities. The present situation as regards young people, if it continues, could create strong social tension with important repercussions of society as a whole.[5]

TABLE 2.2
Young Population

	1960		1980		2000	
	Millions	% of the Population	Millions	% of the Population	Millions	% of the Population
Developed countries	144	28	192	23	176	16
Developing countries	371	72	665	77	893	84
TOTAL	515	100	857	100	1069	100

Source: ILO, Report of the Director General, p. 9.

TABLE 2.3
Youth Unemployment, 1980
(as a percentage of total unemployed)

Thailand	73.9	United States	45.7
India	67.2	Sweden	42.4
Italy	62.4	United Kingdom	42.2
Venezuela	58.2	France	42.1
Spain	57.5	Belgium	38.0
Australia	55.9	Norway	35.9
Philippines	54.9	Denmark	27.9
Turkey	48.6	Germany, Fed. Rep. of	27.3
Portugal	47.4	Switzerland	23.5
Israel	46.6	Japan	21.9

Source: ILO, *Report of the Director General*, p. 16.

THE PRESENT COST OF UNEMPLOYMENT

Unemployment imposes the burden of unemployment assistance on governmental budgets. Undoubtedly, this assistance is socially indispensable, for without it it would be impossible to avoid manifestations of violence.

The unemployment assistance, however, has important consequences not only for governmental budgets, but also for economic activity and for inflation. Let us first examine the amounts devoted to unemployment insurance.

It is difficult to calculate the amount of unemployment benefits with precision, because the system of allocations differs significantly among countries. According to a study by the Commission of European Community, an unemployed father of two children receives approximately 3,100 French francs per month in Belgium and the Federal Republic of Germany, or 37,200 French francs per year. These estimates indicate that the annual cost of unemployment in the countries of the European Community is approximately 380 billion French francs or about $55 billion.

Actually this amount significantly understates the real situation. In France alone, where the number of unemployed is more than 2 million, total allocations for unemployment insurance in 1982 are estimated at 74 billion French francs or about $10 billion.[6] As regards the United Kingdom, a specialized review estimates that the total cost of unemployment insurance for 1982 alone would be £12.4 billion or $22 billion.[7]

In the United States, it was estimated that, at the end of 1981, the cost of unemployment insurance was $80 billion or 560 billion French francs. Were total U.S. unemployment to reach 10 million by the end of 1982, total unemployment benefits would reach $100 billion or 700 billion francs.

The conclusion thus emerges that at present the total benefits being paid by the industrial countries of the West approach an amount of 200 billion U.S. dollars in a single year, an amount higher than the sum of aggregate deficits of all non-oil-producing countries during the three years 1980, 1981, and 1982 combined.

Total Annual Loss of Revenue for OECD Countries: $350 billion

If the overall loss of revenue to the state is calculated, bearing in mind the fact that unemployment benefits are often exempt from taxes and social security contributions, the total burden would exceed a minimum of $200 billion a year. No one can deny the economic and social benefits that industrial countries would have enjoyed if this enormous sum was used for productive investments. And in such a case the original investment expenditure would have been augmented by the multiplier effect. Using as an average multiplier the value of 1.75 proposed by the OECD,[8] it may be estimated that the total direct and indirect loss of revenue for the industrial countries involved is $350 billion a year. This figure coincides with a recent estimate by the OECD. According to that organization, the loss attributed to unemployment would be $340 billion for all of the OECD countries in 1981.[9]

Thus, unemployment assistance constitutes a serious obstacle to the revival of economic activity. To stop unemployment benefits under present conditions would certainly be impossible, as it would lead to social revolution. But to continue them (and they certainly will be continued) can only bring increasing burdens on the budgets of every country, to the detriment of other state expenditures, particularly those for development. Indeed, a grave crisis may be feared if unemployment continues to grow. If this major problem is not solved, it will certainly be impossible for the world economy to emerge from the present crisis.

THE GLOBAL LACK OF PRODUCTIVE INVESTMENT AS THE MAJOR CAUSE OF UNEMPLOYMENT

As long as the present economic stagnation continues, unemployment will not cease to grow. As already stated, it will continue to grow in the coming years.

Besides the demographic factor, that is, the arrival on the labor market of a large number of new job seekers, especially in Europe, the main cause of unemployment seems to be of a structural nature and, in particular, to be the result of long-lasting economic and technological factors. Indeed, the principal cause of unemployment is the insufficiency of productive investments, particularly since 1974, a trend that has been further accentuated since 1979.

The behavior of investments in the industrial world (excluding socialist countries) in recent years confirms the theory that the lack of sufficient inducements to rational investments is the principal cause of the present economic disorder.

In recent economic history, the periods of stagnation have always been marked by a low rate of capital formation. During the great crisis of the 1930s the rate of net capital formation in the United States had fallen to an annual average of 1.4 percent of the national income in the period 1929-30, compared with 10 percent in 1921-39 and 15 percent prior to 1914.[10]

More recently, according to the study of a major Swiss bank,[11] the total volume of investment in the 12 industrial countries has, in the years 1975 and 1976, been some $200 billion less than the amount that would have been reached if total investments had moved upward according to past trends.

If we consider the average multiplier effect applicable, this reduction in investment has caused a total loss of $350 billion in the expansion of national income for the 12 industrial countries in the two years 1975 and 1976 alone. Since that time, the investment situation has become more acute. According to the *World Bank's World Development Report for 1978*, page 93, the average annual rate of growth in gross internal investment was 5.7 percent in the decade 1960-70, compared with only 0.7 percent for the period 1970-76.

As long as businessmen hesitate to undertake new investments to increase the productive potential of their enterprises because they are not confident of their ability to sell the products on the market, this problem will persist and bring about a downward spiral of economic activity, as the negative effects of the multiplier begin to accumulate over time. The magnitude of the investment decline in the main OECD countries is given in Table 2.4.

In addition to the decline in productive investments, a great part of the investments made in various countries has been devoted to purposes that are not directly productive. By far the greatest portion of these nonproductive investments has been in armaments; this problem will be examined in a later chapter.

TABLE 2.4
Productive Investments of Enterprises
in Some Industrial Countries

Countries	average annual growth rate (in percent)		
	1960-73	1973-79	1981
United States	5.7	2.8	2.5
Japan	14.0	1.7	1.6
Fed. Rep. of Germany	4.7	2.4	−2.1
France	7.2	1.4	−2.3
United Kingdom	4.1	3.2	−1.8
Italy	4.7	−1.3	−2.5
Canada	5.8	5.0	6.9
Sweden	4.3	−0.5	−14.0

Source: Banque des Règlements Internationaux, *Rapport*, 1982, p. 31.

TECHNOLOGY-INDUCED UNEMPLOYMENT

The introduction of labor-saving technologies is an important aim of investments today. As regards agriculture in the United States, for example, productive improvements in that sector have radically changed the size of the rural population that constitute the part of the labor force making a living directly from agriculture. This population declined from more than 50 percent living on the land before 1940 to less than 5 percent working in agriculture today, while production in agriculture more than doubled during the same period. Productivity gains in agriculture have thus transformed the social structure.

At the present time also, there is a revolution of similar proportions taking place within the manufacturing sector. For example, labor engaged in the manufacturing production work force in the United States accounts for just 20 percent of the total. Yet as more automated production techniques are introduced into the nation's factories, it will be possible to achieve the same volume of production without an expansion of the work force. A more likely outcome is that the work force in manufacturing will decline as a result of automation and increased international specialization. This revolution will have a major impact on the world economy and will pose major challenges to economic policy. Today, some 40 Japanese auto workers produce the same number of cars as 100 auto workers in one of the older plants in the United States. In five years, it is expected that the same output will be produced by only 12 Japanese workers.

It is a fact that Pakistan engineers now produce architectural drawings for overnight transmission to construction companies in the United States, that Indian computer programmers produce software for overnight transmission to computer companies in the United States, and that English-speaking Koreans are employed to make abstracts of U.S. law cases for inclusion in a data base.

Consequences of Technological Progress

Modern electronics already has a profound effect on production of goods and services and is sure to further profoundly affect the kind of goods and services produced, how they are produced, and where they are produced.

Over the next ten years, modern electronics will accelerate automation, particularly as industrial robots are likely to take over many of the more routine assembly-line functions. Sales of industrial robots are expected to grow by 30 to 35 percent a year. Over a ten-year period, this should have a major worldwide impact on manufacturing. Countries in which the large-scale investments required for automated production facilities are made will gain a significant competitive advantage in this process and a number of important consequences can already be anticipated:

• There will be fewer production jobs on the assembly lines and more jobs in supportive services such as machine design, computer programming, and maintenance services.

• An abundant supply of labor and low wages will become less of an advantage in manufacturing, but will remain an advantage in many service industries. This is because labor will become a smaller input into the physical production of goods but at the same time there is likely to be a larger demand for services.

• The location of production facilities will be progressively more separated from the locus where new techniques, methods, and products are developed.

The negative impact of technology on the employment of labor in the main industrial countries is in evidence.

A Dual Problem

A problem that is dual in nature confronts the world economy: there is, on one hand, a lack of sufficient demand that leads to capacity underutilization of existing plant and equipment; and, on the other hand, a substitution, technologically imposed, of capital for labor that has accelerated in recent years. Even if demand were to recover, the technologically imposed labor substitution effect would remain as a structural parameter in the world economy, thereby continuously displacing labor in production. Thus, the additions to the labor force, shown for the main industrial countries, deter-

mined by demographic factors, may be added to an ever-growing
army of unemployed. This situation seems likely to become permanent in nature. Permanent, that is, unless the *modus operandi* of the
economic system were to change in a significant and fundamental
way. Needless to say, of course, the same situation, but even more
aggravated by the demographic factor, exists in the developing
countries. The theorems that emerge from the analysis, so far, are:

First, as the technological revolution in manufacturing, like the
technological revolution in agriculture that preceded it, displaces
workers, these workers are absorbed either by the service sector or
become unemployed. To the extent that they are absorbed by the
service sector, and the service sector expands as a proportion of the
economy, a permanent and continuous inflationary tendency that
can be expected to operate with permanent and irreversible force
is built in the economy itself.

Second, to the extent that these displaced workers become a
permanent army of unemployed, further structural budgetary
problems may ensue that lock the country into further stagnation,
thus aggravating inflation via government deficits.

Third, such deficits lead, in turn, either to accomodating monetary policy, with ensuing inflationary consequences; or, to a conservative monetary posture with rising interest rates, more inflation,
and, progressively, the full gamut of the "crowding out" effects in
the financial markets.

All of the above cases are characterized by rising unemployment,
stagnating investment, and the export of technological innovations —
as production in domestic markets, after a time, becomes highly
uncompetitive.

Producing More with Less Labor:
a Fact or an Optical Illusion?

Figure 2.3 relates output to employment in the manufacturing
sector of some of the OECD countries. The graphs making up this
figure can be thought of as analogous to the traditional "production
possibility curves," except that in this case, instead of single years,
they show five-year moving averages for levels of output and employ-

FIGURE 2.3
Employment and Output in Manufacturing
(1975 = 100)

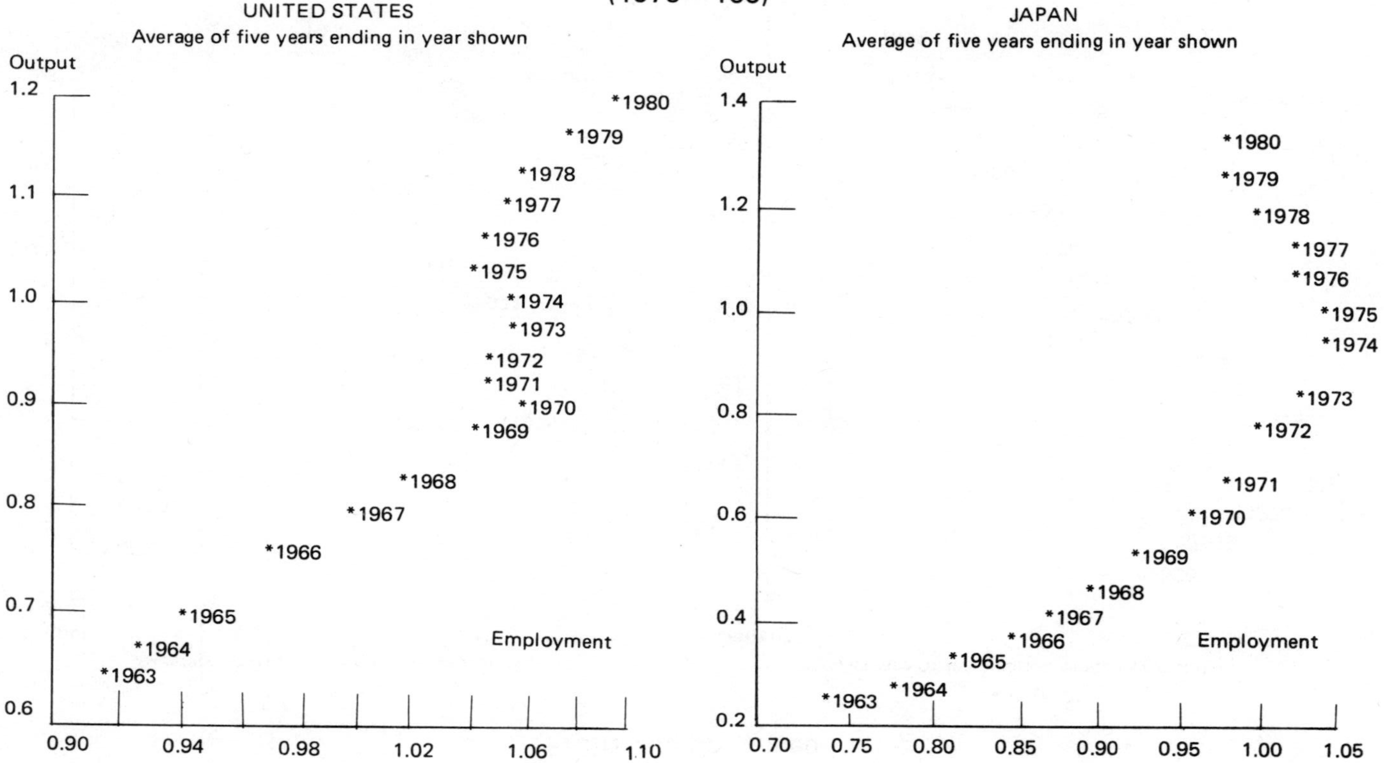

UNITED STATES
Average of five years ending in year shown

JAPAN
Average of five years ending in year shown

35

Figure 2.3, Continued

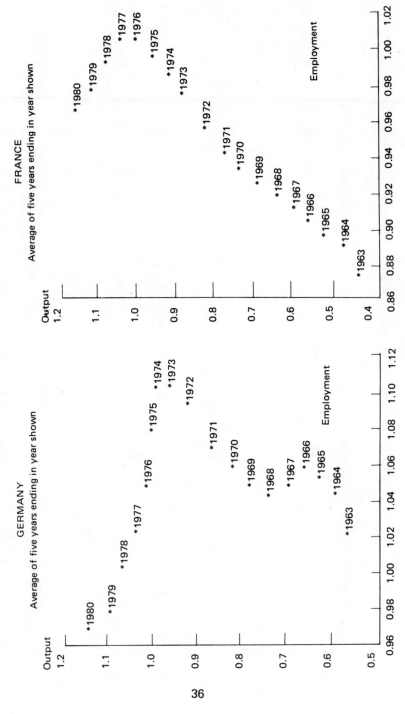

GERMANY
Average of five years ending in year shown

FRANCE
Average of five years ending in year shown

36

Figure 2.3, Continued

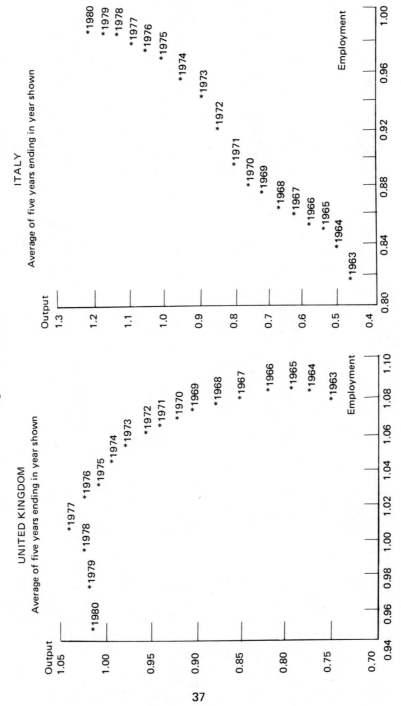

Figure 2.3, Continued

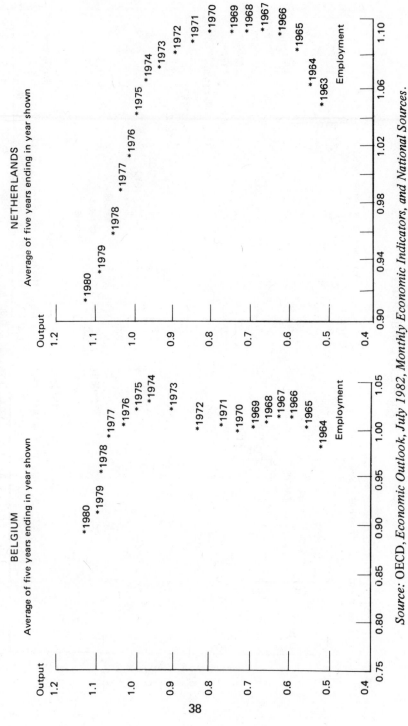

Source: OECD, *Economic Outlook, July 1982, Monthly Economic Indicators, and National Sources.*

FIGURE 2.4
Unemployment and Capacity Use in the United States

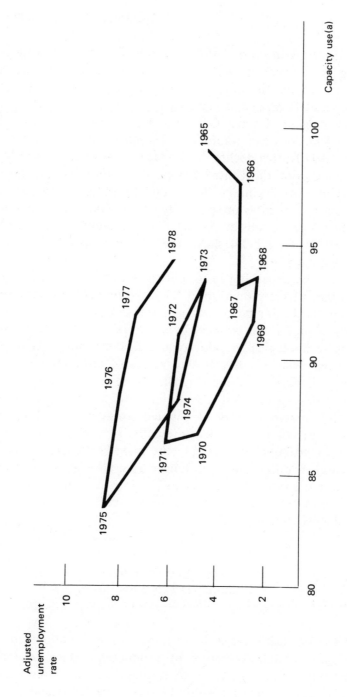

(a) Total private non-farm sector.

ment, covering the period 1963 to 1980. The use of moving averages, ending in the year shown at each point on the graphs, was used in order to remove the influence of transitory phenomena that might have operated during a particular year.

For Belgium, France, Germany, Japan, the Netherlands, and the United Kingdom the graphs reveal a *fall* in employment starting in the mid-1970s; this decline took place while further *gains* in output were made. For the United States, the graph does not show a fall in employment beginning in the mid-1970s as for the other countries, but it does show progressively smaller additions to employment for the same expansion in output in relation to the 1960s and early 1970s. Figure 2.4 shows the unemployment and capacity use in the United States.[12]

Thus, the expansion in output since the mid-1970s is associated, over time, with a reduction in the labor inputs. This may very well portend the beginning of a negative long-term trend favoring other factors of production at the expense of labor. Whether this substitution is technologically induced and further reinforced by changes in the real relative costs of the factors of production, particularly at times of near-economic stagnation and modest output gains, or whether this substitution is predominantly a technological phenomenon, is a matter worthy of detailed consideration. However, even on the basis of the evidence presented here alone, it may not be premature to conclude that (1) the main bottleneck in the way of expansion in output may no longer be skilled labor, as in the past, but capital; and (2) to the extent possible, capital expansion in the future must be of an employment-increasing rather than an employment-decreasing nature.

Labor and Energy:
Complements or Substitutes?

This conclusion raises the question of the relationship between labor and capital as factors of production. More generally, can capital expansion that is of an employment-increasing nature also be of an energy-saving nature? In short, are labor and energy substitutable or complementary factors of production?

To the extent that evidence on this point exists, it can be only of a preliminary nature. Changes in the nature of capital take place only slowly over time, and the critical event, the first oil shock, which drastically changed the relative cost of energy inputs, took place less than a decade ago.

Preliminary as it might be, the existing evidence suggests the following:

• In the case of the United States, in 18 out of 20 individual subsectors of manufacturing, and for the manufacturing sector as a whole, *capital has been a complement to energy* for the period 1960 to 1970. But in 14 out of the same 20 subsectors and for the manufacturing sector as a whole, *capital has been a substitute* during the period 1970 to 1978.

• In the case of France, the United Kingdom, Canada, and the Federal Republic of Germany, capital and energy were found to be also predominantly substitutes in most of the same 20 subsectors of manufacturing examined, as well as for the manufacturing sector as a whole.

• In the case of Japan, substitution between energy and capital was found to exist only in the case of 2 manufacturing subsectors, but for the remaining 18 manufacturing subsectors the degree of complementarity between capital and energy has been declining since 1973.

These findings address the question of the relationship between labor and capital only indirectly. It would appear inevitable, however, that, to the extent that capital and energy are substitutes, capital and labor will largely be complementary. While this does not negate the fact that technologically induced substitution of labor has been taking place, it does emphasize that to the extent that economies move progressively toward energy-saving equipment the displacement of labor will be less than it might have otherwise been.

More Output with 15 Million Fewer Workers!

We may conclude thus by saying that to a large extent the backward-sloping production possibility curves were due to the low level of output that characterized the post-1973 era and that, among other things, might have induced firms to reduce variable costs (labor) to the minimum; to a large extent this was also due to the introduction of more capital-extensive (and therefore less labor-extensive) methods of production. But in the longer run, as the findings presented in this chapter suggest, to the extent that capital equipment becomes progressively more energy-saving, the technological substitution of labor by other factors of production will be less than it would have been in the absence of such energy-saving capital.

Still, however, between 1978 and 1982, the number of unemployed in the OECD countries increased from 15 million to more than 33 million, while aggregate production diminished rather than expanded. In other words, with 15 million workers no longer employed, total production increased by 2 percent.

This situation alone, and without even carrying it to its ultimate conclusion, demands immediate reconsideration of the social policies now in effect, particularly since the demographic statistics project a continuous increase in the number of new entrants to the global labor force.

NOTES

1. OECD, *Economic Outlook*, various issues.
2. OECD, *Observer*, July 1982.
3. International Labor Office, *Report of the Director General*, 68th session (Geneva, 1982), pp. 8 and 9).
4. ILO, *Report of the Director General*, p. 15.
5. A bibliography of studies on the problem of the employment of young people has been published by the OECD: *Youth Employment* (Paris, 1980).
6. See *Le Monde*, September 22, 1982. According to the same source, the cost of unemployment expenditure in 1983 is expected to be in the range of 90-95 billion French francs.
7. According to the British Manpower Services Commission, the annual cost per unemployed person is £4,300, which corresponds to about 27,200 French francs.
8. According to a recent study, the average multiplier for the OECD countries is approximately 2.0 (Bert Hickman and Victor Filatov, *On a Decomposition of International Income Multipliers* [Philadelphia, Pa.: University of

Pennsylvania, 1981], unpublished manuscript).

9. OECD, *Observer*, no. 115 (March 1982).

10. United Nations, *Survey of the Economic Situation of Europe in 1949*, (Geneva, 1950), p. 229.

11. Union Bank of Switzerland, *Business Facts and Figures*, 1978.

12. OECD, *Economic Survey* (Paris, July 1982), p. 28.

MILITARY EXPENDITURES IN RELATION
TO NATIONAL PRODUCT

Military expenditures may be considered as being useful, and even productive in the sense that they provide a means of defending a country from external harm. They also constitute a collective effort that can indeed help strengthen the productive apparatus of a country. But this is only true if the volume of military expenditures forms a reasonable share of the governmental budget and is in harmony with the total expenditures of a nation.

When expenditures on armaments and military defense go beyond certain limits they are detrimental to economic and social progress. They are unproductive in the true economic sense, since the goods produced do not in turn produce other goods useful to maintain the standards of living of the population. Furthermore, armament must, after a relatively short time, be replaced by more sophisticated equipment reflecting better, new technological developments and military strategies. We thus witness a waste of wealth, which, if utilized for other purposes, could have beneficial repercussions on economic and social progress.

45

As Professor Lawrence R. Klein has observed, "War spending, whether it is domestic or foreign, is never productive in a conventional economic sense. The large-scale military buildup produced a great deal of hardware — tanks, planes, missiles, electronic gear, weapons — but little of it had a useful economic life."[1] This nonproductive utilization of an important part of national resources leads to a decline in productivity growth. The starting of the present inflationary experience in the United States was, according to Lawrence Klein, "the beginning of the escalation of the war in Vietnam at 1965."

When we look at the evolution of military expenditures between 1973 and 1979 we note that their increase has been almost parallel to the increase of national product. The ratio of military expenditures to GNP for the world as a whole (except the socialist countries) has remained at the same level, 5.9 percent in 1973, 5.7 percent in 1977, and 5.8 percent in 1979.[2] For the countries of the Warsaw Pact, the ratio of military expenditures, according to the same U.S. publication, was slightly reduced between 1973 and 1977, but it was at a level almost double that of the Western countries (12.1 to 11.7 percent of GNP).

In recent years, the increase in military expenditures has been more rapid than that of the gross national product. In 1980-82, while the world economy continued to be in deep recession with a growth rate of about 1 percent, military expenditures showed a much higher growth rate. According to the President's Economic Report to Congress, military expenditures will probably increase between 1981 and 1986 by 9 percent annually in real terms. Their percentage share of the total federal expenditures, which was 23.7 percent in 1981, will be 35.4 percent in 1986.[3]

If, at the same time, an increase of 3 percent in military expenditures in real terms is to be applied by other NATO countries, on the basis of a recent decision of the NATO Council, the economic situation will deteriorate, since this increase would be almost double or triple the real increase expected in national income. This arms race will no doubt be continued also by the Warsaw Pact countries. In the Soviet Union, according to estimates by Wharton Econometric Forecasting Associates, defense expenditures accounted for 14 percent of total GNP or 24.3 percent of consumption in 1981, and are expected to increase by 5 percent annually, reaching 16 percent of GNP, or 29 percent of consumption, in 1986.[4] Such militarization would constitute the greatest danger for world peace, as well as for the rest of the world economy. Often the military burden is even higher as military expenditures are traditionally understated. Expenses for science and research are frequently used as a "cover up" for military purposes.

A special committee of experts of the United Nations has examined and produced a long series of reports on the problem of disarmament. According to these documents, it has been ascertained that the military industry is not a long-term agent of economic growth and that budget deficits arising from military expenditures provoke a double inflationary pressure.

The effects are more unfavorable in developing countries. Generally the military research constitutes in the end a grave waste and the results obtained are not utilized for productive purposes.

According to the United Nations, an amount of $1 billion utilized in the private sector, could create employment for 25-30,000 people, more than if this amount were to be used for arms. In the developing countries, the gap is larger. Although, in these countries the cost of one job in a military enterprise is $20,000 the cost of one job in the agricultural sector is only $150.[5]

Moreover, military expenditures draw heavily on the manpower of young people just at the time of their lives when training should be improved and broadened and their rates of productivity should be rising. Instead their excessive specialization in the arms industry makes them very difficult to reemploy in the private sector.

ENORMOUS MILITARY EXPENDITURES
BURDEN THE THIRD WORLD

It is not only the developed countries that make large military expenditures. The developing countries also devote important sums to such purposes, and these sums continue to increase more rapidly than their national incomes, at the expense of economic development priorities.

Figure 3.1, two diagrams prepared by the Stockholm International Peace Research Institute (SIPRI), reproduced here, indicate

FIGURE 3.1

Distribution of World Military Expenditure, 1971 and 1980

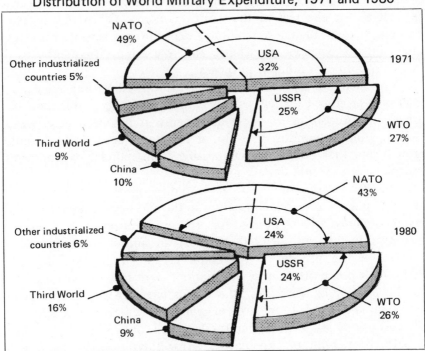

Source: SIPRI, *World Armaments and Disarmament Yearbook 1980*, (London: Taylor & Frances, 1980).

the share distribution of total military expenditures between 1971 and 1980 by groups of countries. It appears that in 1980 the share of the United States fell from 32 percent to 24 percent whereas that of the USSR only fell from 25 percent in 1971 to 24 percent in 1980. This is due to the tremendous increase in the military expenditures of the countries of the Third World; their share increased from 9 percent of world military expenditure in 1971, to 16 percent in 1980.[6]

For many of these developing countries the share of military expenditures in their total public expenditures goes far beyond the corresponding share in the developed countries. The Arab countries and some others in the Third World are seeking to strengthen their arsenals with arms that are increasingly costly as a result of technological advances. Thus, the countries of the Middle East, whose ratio of military expenditures to their GNP was 7.7 percent in 1968, reached a figure of 14.2 percent in 1976, and this has been steadily increasing.

This accumulation of armaments in the Third World countries has provoked, as the *Willy Brandt Report* states, a "growing instability and a barrier to their development."[7] The race to increase armaments continuously in order to attain ever-stronger power exceeded $80 billion for the Third World countries in 1980. Unlike the industrial countries, developing countries have no independent arms industries; they therefore have to import their arms, thereby devoting a part of their export proceeds to the purpose. In 1980, arms imports absorbed 33 percent of their export proceeds, and in 1981 they absorbed 37 percent.

Third World Conflicts Since 1945

According to SIPRI, about 130 wars or armed conflicts have taken place in the Third World since 1945, and 50 of them took place during the past decade.[8] All these armed conflicts were fought exclusively in the Third World with weapons supplied by the industrial countries. The United States and the Soviet Union are the major suppliers for some 75 percent of the arms exported. Figure 3.2, also reproduced from the SIPRI publication mentioned above, represents military world export, by countries, and imports, by region, during the period 1977-80.

The largest share of arms exports is directed toward the Middle East countries; their imports are 32 percent of the world's total. Among the main exporters of armaments, the United States is first with 43.3 percent of the total and a value of $27.7 billion annually for the 1970-80 period. The USSR is second with 27.4 percent of the total and a value of $16.8 billion. France is in the third place and the Federal Republic of Germany is also among the main exporters.

In the period 1979-81 the Soviet Union overtook the United States due to the big increase in arms export to India, to Cuba, and to countries of the Middle East and North Africa and to the decline in U.S. exports after the policy of restraint adopted by President Carter in 1977. However in July 1981 this policy of restraint on

FIGURE 3.2
Shares of World Exports (by Country) and
World Imports (by Region) of Major Weapons
1977-80*

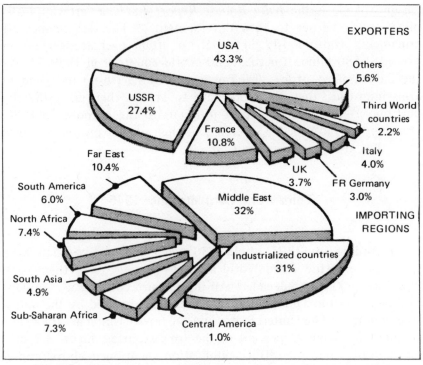

*The values include licenses sold for the production of major weapons.

Source: SIPRI, *Brochure*, 1982, p. 9.

arms sales was abandoned and the sale of arms has become a major instrument of foreign policy for the United States.[9]

DOES THE ECONOMIC "FALLOUT" FROM MILITARY EXPENDITURES FOSTER ECONOMIC GROWTH?

It may be argued that there is an economic "fallout" from military (and space) research. This is true, but there is evidence that this "fallout" is relatively small and that it does not necessarily produce economic growth.

The *Brooks Report* of the OECD emphasizes that the correlation between military expenditures and economic growth appears to be negative and it adds that the predominance of military research leads to an economic disequilibrium, adversely affecting production for peaceful purposes.[10]

The example of Japan, which has become a great economic and industrial power, provides an important argument in favor of the thesis that low expenditures on armaments favor economic growth. In Japan military expenditures have not exceeded, during the decades of the 1960s and 1970s, 1 percent of the GNP, as indicated in Table 3.1 below, but the country achieved a very high growth rate in this period. The average annual growth rate of GNP was 10.5 percent for the 1960-70 period.

On the other hand, other countries, and the United States in particular, as Table 3.1 indicates, with military expenditures at a rate 5 times higher than that of Japan, showed very limited growth and a large amount of unemployment. Japan was able to use a large part of its GNP thus saved to modernize and develop its productive apparatus. The result was that Japan — helped also by other favorable internal factors such as the cost of labor and its organizational system — through its continuously increasing exports is today a formidable economic competitor of the other industrialized countries of the West.

TABLE 3.1
Military Expenditures
as a Percentage of GNP

	1960	1970	1975	1979	1981
Japan	1.1	0.8	0.9	0.9	0.9
Fed. Rep. Germany	4.0	3.3	3.6	3.3	3.2
U.S.A.	9.0	8.0	6.0	5.2	5.5
France	6.5	4.2	3.8	4.0	3.9
U.K.	6.5	4.8	5.0	4.9	5.1

Source: Japan Institute for Social and Economic Affairs, *An International Comparison*, 1982, p. 73.

The same is true for the Federal Republic of Germany, although its military expenditures are about 3.2 percent of GNP as compared with 5.5 percent for the United States. However, one must take into account that a large part of the total military expenditures of the Federal Republic of Germany covers the expenses for stationing on its territory of Allied Military Forces (wages, rents, etc.) thereby limiting the amount devoted to armaments.

As a result of the destruction caused by the war, the Federal Republic of Germany and Japan have been able to renew and develop their productive apparatus very intensively. They are now competing strongly in the export area. This gives these countries a very great economic advantage, associated as we have noted with a relatively small inflation rate. Paradoxically, the countries victorious in the Second World War are now in a disadvantageous position. But, to a large extent, the growth of the economic power of Japan and the Federal Republic of Germany may be explained, as we have seen, by their relatively low levels of arms expenditures.

Has Military Antagonism
Led to the Scientific-Technical Revolution?

Undoubtedly, the scientific-technical revolution of our time would not have taken place, or at least not at so fast a pace, had military factors and the race for military superiority between the blocs in the East and West not occurred. If the world were not divided, nuclear energy, satellite communications, and telematics would probably not have been developed and applied in industry as rapidly as they were. Furthermore, space travel and the use of space would not have occurred as early in time.

It is paradoxical that most of the investments made by the State are for armaments, while entrepreneurs hesitate to make new investments. Furthermore, the fear of increasing unemployment during a period of recession causes the industrial countries to hesitate to cut back on the production and export of armaments. It is also relevant to note that even political leaders who were hitherto hostile to any expansion of arms exports are beginning to reason differently, while workers in the armaments industries demand maintenance of their employment through the development of the arms industries and arms exports. Thus, the expansion of arms production and sales takes on increasing dimensions and creates unfavorable repercussions for other economic sectors, and for the world as a whole.

Defense and Nondefense Expenditures

The above notwithstanding, according to an empirical study by Professor Bela Balassa, between 1962 and 1979 the United States continued to increase its comparative advantage in technology-intensive products, but during approximately the same period, defense expenditures on research and development (R & D) as percent of GNP fell more than one-half between 1963 and 1975 alone, while nondefense expenditures increased.[11] Thus even in the presence of rapidly declining defense expenditures on R & D, the United States strengthened its specialization for technology-intensive products, which also explains, according to the author, the high income elasticity of demand for U.S. exports.

These comparisons suggest that R & D defense expenditures were not positively correlated, at least during this period, with the strengthening of the technological superiority of U.S. technology-intensive products. This result is not counterintuitive if it is realized that defense expenditures on research and development have quite a different effect on the structure of the economy than research and development expenditures by the private sector do.

Profit considerations in the private sector lead to R & D spending that has high productivity and contributes, therefore, to noninflationary economic growth directly, while defense expenditures are oriented toward improving military preparedness alone. Such expenditures contribute to economic growth only through their indirect effects, that is, to the extent that income received from such activities is spent in nondefense industries. As such the contribution to economic growth is both slow and inflationary — inflationary because while such defense expenditures add potentially to private aggregate demand, they do nothing to add on the other side of the equation to private aggregate supply.

FROM THE "CONSUMER ECONOMY"
TO THE "ARMS RACE ECONOMY"?

High military expenditures such as those that have taken place since 1975 reduce to a great extent investments aimed at production of consumer goods, upset the balance between supply and demand, and provoke inflation and unemployment.

This armament race endangers the existence of humankind as a whole. Instead of directing man's activity toward the creation of ethical, political, economic, and social values, it leads it to the creation of destructive forces. Is it necessary to recall that two-thirds of research expenditures are for military purposes? That the world — West and East — spends $600 billion each year, that is a million dollars each minute, for military purposes? What a waste of resources at a time when one-fifth of the population of the globe suffers from hunger and malnutrition and lives in complete poverty!

There is no doubt that the real path to security in the world lies in economic development, for misery and poverty are factors of insecurity for everyone. The more the world depends on the production of arms, the more insecure it is. Furthermore, especially in a recession, the armaments race brings with it an economic crisis that gravely harms and endangers all countries in the world.

War, an Unthinkable Eventuality in the Atomic Age

Ever since the August 1945 explosions of the first two atomic bombs at Hiroshima and Nagasaki, numerous thermonuclear experiments, conducted especially by the two superpowers, have shown the destructive power of these instruments. In fact, we have reached a stage at which war would be a veritable disaster — in fact would mean suicide — for the whole of humanity.

Since the time of the late Indian prime minister, Pandit Nehru, who stressed that "war has become an inconceivable eventuality in the atomic age," there have been repeated warnings by experts and other qualified personalities on the consequences of nuclear warfare; these experts have called on those responsible to make a decision on this crucial problem. This indecision constitutes the greatest risk for mankind, as Gordon Dean predicted some 30 years ago. The former chairman of the U.S. Atomic Energy Commission wrote in 1953, without being aware of the subsequent progress of thermo-nuclear energy: "The atomic age has introduced a new factor that must be taken into the calculations. Whereas before the problem was simply one of war or peace, it is now one of oblivion or peace. With a question like this, it is hard to imagine any answer except peace. Yet man, even in the atomic age, has not chosen peace. He also has not chosen oblivion, and he seems to think he can go on forever without deciding upon one or the other. Maybe he can, but the risks are enormous."[12]

Thirty years have elapsed since Gordon Dean's warning and the two superpowers continue to remain undecided on the road to choose, and prefer an armaments race, to which they devote enormous expenditures, to the detriment of their own economic and social progress and that of other countries. The experts tell us that a war in which hydrogen bombs were used would result in such destruction that there would be no victor, for even the so-called victorious country would be transformed into a chaotic slaughterhouse. Scientists estimate that if all the nuclear weapons in the world, which for the United States, Russia, Great Britain, France, China, and India amount to 43,000, were detonated, the force would be equal to 10 trillion tons of nuclear explosive power.[13]

To understand the significance of this explosive power one need only recall that the Hiroshima bomb was of only 2,000 tons.

The Balance of Power
and the Race for Superiority

Under such conditions, are there truly people who can envisage the launching of an atomic war? Undoubtedly the existence of a balance of power constitutes a guarantee for avoiding nuclear warfare. However, a "balance of power" is a relative notion. From the moment that each of the two antagonistic blocs has sufficient means, as they do at present, to annihilate the principal cities of its adversary, each has a more or less equal offensive and destructive power. The pursuit of a course for "supremacy" of one over the other serves nothing. The existence of a certain number of hydrogen bombs in the hands of each of the two camps is sufficient to prevent the outbreak of total war.

The continued arms race for the purpose of obtaining superiority is "empty of meaning" according to George F. Kennan, former U.S. Ambassador to the Soviet Union and architect of the U.S. policy of containing Soviet expansion. In an interview with *U.S. News and World Report*, responding to the question "if the Soviet Union could become dangerous when they attain a clear military superiority," George Kennan said:

> First of all, the Soviet Union is not going to attain *usable* superiority. In reality, the truly perilous time will come not when Moscow feels very strong but when it feels very weak. Desperate people behave in a far more foolish and reckless way than those who are riding along quite well. Kremlin leaders are more likely to lash out if they conclude that their authority in Eastern Europe − or over Russia itself − is unavailing.[14]

The same thesis has been expounded by such other eminent U.S. personalities as McGeorge Bundy, Robert S. McNamara and Gerald Smith.[15]

These statements further reinforce the view that military expenditures at the levels at which they currently stand, not to mention the levels at which they are expected to progress, are, from a strategic point of view, unnecessary as well as counterproductive; and that instead of safeguarding world peace by offsetting strength among the superpowers, they may in fact invite a nuclear war.

However, there is a controversy about the so-called military superiority between the two superpowers that affects the present and the future arms policy. President Reagan claims that "today in virtually every measure of military power, the Soviet Union enjoys a decided advantage." From the other side, Soviet leader Yuri Andropov denies that Russia has an advantage and asserts: "The allegation of a 'lag' behind the USSR which the Americans must close is a deliberate untruth."[16]

This disagreement about the comparative strength of the two superpowers constitutes a dangerous lack of mutual trust and can lead to disaster. The problem becomes more acute as a result of the difficulty in measuring usable military power in the nuclear age.

From an economic point of view, particularly of stagnation or slow growth in the world economy continues and military expenditures also continue to increase at projected rates, an ever-larger proportion of the world's output will be used for the arms race. As stated earlier, on the basis of current projections, military expenditures will account for no less than 30 percent of the entire anticipated increase in the GNP of the United States between 1981 and 1987. This, in turn, means that the U.S. federal budget will account for, and become the source of, no less than 82 percent of the total anticipated *change* in the national product in that period. And as also stated earlier, defense expenditures in the USSR will have reached 29 percent of consumption in 1986 and will continue to grow at twice the annual rate of consumption.

In the countries of the Third World, where arms imports as share of total exports increased by four percentage points within a single year, from 34 percent in 1980 to 37 percent in 1981, it will take only a few years at this rate before arms imports exceed more than half of the value of their exports.

Such developments, were they to continue for the rest of the decade, would inexorably bring about the end of the "consumer economy" and its transformation to the "arms race economy."

Are we aware of the problems and consequences of such a development?

NOTES

1. Lawrence R. Klein, "Two decades of U.S. Economic Policy and Present Prospects, A view from the outside," paper delivered at the Conference on Economic Policies in the U.S., September 1981, in Paris.

2. See U.S. Arms Control Agency, *World Military Expenditures 1968-1977*, (Washington D.C., October 1979), p. 27. For 1979, the estimate is the author's.

3. *Economic Report of the President to Congress*, February 1982, p. 83.

4. Wharton Econometric Forecasting Associates, *"Centrally Planned Economies Outlook,"* April 1982, table, page 37.

5. Andre Trotter, United Nations, "Un fardeau écrasant," in *Le Monde*, December 20, 1982.

6. SIPRI, *World Armaments and Disarmament Yearbook 1980* (London: Taylor and Francis, 1980), p. XVIII.

7. Brandt Commission, *North-South — A Program for Survival*, Paris, 1980, p. 205. See also: André Fontaine: *Un seul lit pour deux rêves. Histoire de la "détente" 1962-1981*, Paris, Fayard 1981.

8. SIPRI, *Brochure*, 1981, p. 12.

9. SIPRI, *Brochure*, 1982, p. 9.

10. OECD, *Science, Growth and Society* (Paris 1971). In April 1980 an international meeting on the economic effects of space technology was organized under the auspices of the Parliamentary Assembly of the Council of Europe.

11. Bela Balassa, "The United States in the World Economy," paper delivered at the Conference on "the Political Economy of the United States," September 1981 in Paris, pp. 14-15, tables 8 and 10.

12. Gordon Dean, "Report on the Atom," 1954, p. 265.

13. *U.S. News and World Report*, December 6, 1982.

14. *U.S. News and World Report*, April 26, 1982, p. 18.

15. See *Foreign Affairs, Nuclear Weapons and the Atlantic Alliance*, New York, Spring 1982.

16. *U.S. News and World Report*, January 10, 1983, p. 16. According to the U.S. Department of Defense and the International Institute for Strategic Studies, the repartition of nuclear arms between the two superpowers was the following at the end of 1982:

	United States	USSR
International ballistic missiles	1052	1398
Submarine-launched ballistic missiles	520	950
Long-range strategic bombers	316	150
Total strategic nuclear warheads	9300	7300
Total explosive power — megatons	3000	5000

4

THE OVER-INDEBTEDNESS OF THE THIRD WORLD ENDANGERS THE INTERNATIONAL FINANCIAL SYSTEM

A DISTURBING GAP
BETWEEN RICH AND POOR COUNTRIES

As is well known, there is an unequal distribution of world income and a large gap exists between the rich and poor countries, normally called the Northern and the Southern countries of the World.[1] This gap, which is very great, is an element that aggravates the international economic crisis. "One of the great contradictions of our epoch," states the Willy Brandt Commission in its *Report*, "is that these inequalities exist and even in certain respects are increasing at the very moment when human society is beginning to become aware to what extent its elements are closely linked among one another, just as the North and the South depend on each other in the framework of a single world economy."[2]

Table 4.1 and Figures 4.1 and 4.2 show the inequalities in production and population between industrial, developing, and socialist countries.[3]

The following conclusions may be drawn from this table:

• The developed market economy countries as well as the socialist countries of Eastern Europe (which also belong to the

TABLE 4.1
Participation of Various Groups of
Countries in World Production (GDP) and Population,
1960-80 (in percent)

Country group	1960			1980		
	Population	Total GDP	Ratio of GDP per capita*	Population	Total GDP	Ratio of GDP per capita*
Developed market economy countries	22.9	72.1	1.00	19.4	64.7	1.00
Socialist countries of Eastern Europe	10.6	12.0	0.36	8.8	15.3	0.52
Developing countries including Asia	66.5	15.9	0.08	71.8	20.0	0.09
TOTAL	100.0	100.0		100.0	100.0	

*To that of the Developed market economy countries.

Source: *United Nations, Trade and Development Report 1981*, New York, 1982, p. 90.

FIGURE 4.1
Distribution of World Income, 1980

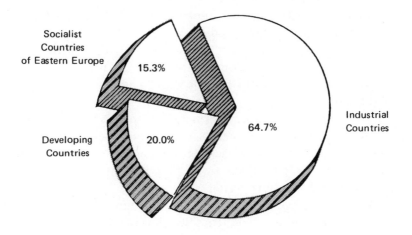

Socialist
Countries
of Eastern Europe   15.3%

Developing
Countries   20.0%

64.7%   Industrial
Countries

Source: Compiled by the author.

FIGURE 4.2
Distribution of World Population, 1980

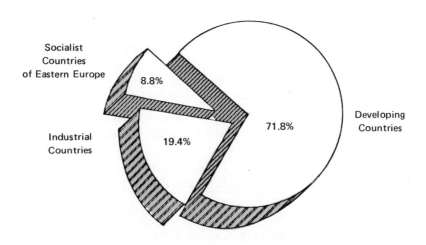

Socialist
Countries
of Eastern Europe   8.8%

Industrial
Countries   19.4%

71.8%   Developing
Countries

Source: Compiled by the author.

category of developed countries), with 28.2 percent of the world's population produced 80 percent of the world's total product in 1980, whereas the developing countries, with 71.8 percent of the world's population, did not produce more than 20 percent of the total product. In particular, the United States alone, with a mere 6 percent of world population, contributed 31 percent to world production. The total world income (GNP) amounted in 1979 to $10,150 billion.[4]

• The developing countries (including socialist Asia) share of the world's total population increased from 66.5 percent in 1960 to 71.8 percent in 1980, whereas the population of the industrial countries of the West declined from 22.9 percent to 19.4 percent of the total during the same period.

• Whereas the percentage share of the gross domestic product (GDP) of developing countries to the world's total improved appreciably during the 20 years in question (from 11.9 percent in 1960 to 14.7 percent in 1980), the ratio of GDP per capita to that of developed countries remained almost unchanged on account of the population explosion in the developing countries.

Absolute Poverty Increases

Thus, despite the more rapid growth of developing countries during this period, their GDP per capita has remained steady, and in fact became appreciably lower in the poorest countries. Forty percent of the world's 800 million destitute and illiterate live in India and their situation has not changed significantly over more than two decades according to the Planning Commission of India. People have perhaps more, but they expect more. Under present conditions, several decades will be needed before a more balanced and equitable distribution of world production is attained.

This inexorable trend may be seen in the fact that at present, with the same growth rate — let us suppose, 3 percent — the annual increase in GDP per capita would be $300 in the rich countries, $45 in the countries with an intermediate income, and a mere $8 in the countries with low income, even though their populations represent half of the world total.[5] This means, therefore, that it would take the developing countries 80 years to attain the present per capita income level of the Western European countries and for the poorest developing countries, which contain one-half of the world's population, about 200 years!

Although the rates of economic growth during the 1950-80 period were more encouraging than was hoped for at the beginning of the period, the number of people living in absolute poverty has not been reduced. The number was 770 million in 1975 and in 1980 went beyond 800 million, according to the World Bank. This figure will rise even further in the coming decades.[6] Some idea of this wide gap may be gained from Table 4.2. Indeed, the difference between the levels of the low-income countries, which represent more than one-half of the world population, and the levels of the high-income countries is enormous. The per capita income is 32 times higher in the developed countries and the average life expectancy is 13 years more than in the low-income countries.

THE DETERIORATION OF THE TERMS OF TRADE AND THE REDUCTION IN PUBLIC ASSISTANCE

The situation of chronic crisis in the non-oil-exporting developing countries has worsened because of two factors that have taken on large dimensions in recent years: (1) the deterioration of their terms of trade; and (2) the reduction in public assistance.

Terms of Trade

The deterioration of the terms of trade of the non-oil-exporting developing countries has been accelerated during the 1973-80 period. In the 1962-72 period, the decline was at a rather moderate average of 1 to 1.5 percent yearly. According to IMF estimates, the loss for these countries in the seven years of the 1973-79 period was $80 billion, which meant a large reduction in their purchasing power. The percentage change of the previous year of the terms of trade is shown in Figure 4.3.

TABLE 4.2
The Development Gap

	Low-Income Countries	Lower-Middle-Income Countries	High-Income Countries
Mid-1981 population (millions)	2,188.6	454.5	1,134.1
Average per capita GNP, 1980 (in dollars)	255	566	8,222
Average birth rate (per 1000)	30	38	16
Average death rate (per 1000)	12	14	9
Average life expectancy (years)	59	53	72
Average infant mortality rate (per 1000 births)	101	98	21
Average per capita education expenditures (in dollars)	9	15	373
Average per capita military expenditures (in dollars)	15	24	310

Source: U.S. Foreign Policy and the Third World Agenda, 1982 (New York: Praeger, 1982).

FIGURE 4.3
Terms of Trade

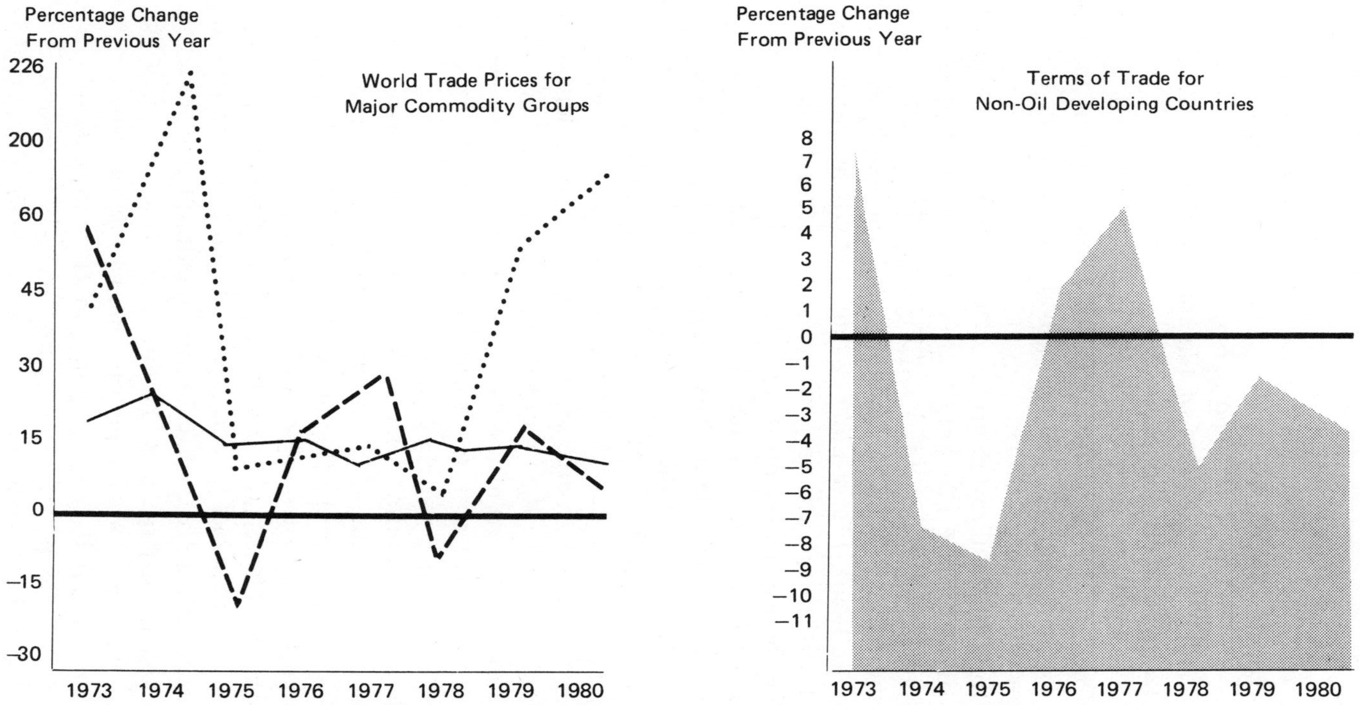

Percentage Change
From Previous Year

World Trade Prices for
Major Commodity Groups

Percentage Change
From Previous Year

Terms of Trade for
Non-Oil Developing Countries

226
200
60
45
30
15
0
−15
−30

1973 1974 1975 1976 1977 1978 1979 1980

8
7
6
5
4
3
2
1
0
−1
−2
−3
−4
−5
−6
−7
−8
−9
−10
−11

1973 1974 1975 1976 1977 1978 1979 1980

· · · · · · Oil   — — — Non-Oil Primary Commodities   ——— Manufactures

Source: International Monetary Fund, *Annual Report*, 1981.

In fact, developing countries remain heavily dependent upon their exports of primary products. More than 60 percent of their exports of food products and agricultural raw materials as well as 80 percent of their exports of minerals and metals are directed to developed market economies.[7]

The proportion of these basic products to total world commerce has greatly decreased following the recession in industrial countries, and prices, in real terms, had reached, at the end of 1980, their lowest level in 30 years.

Efforts to stabilize the prices of basic products and improve the terms of trade have had only limited success. The agreement concluded in June 1980 by the United Nations for the establishment of a common fund for basic products and the resulting agreements known as Lomé 1 and Lomé 2 undoubtedly constitute essential steps for the restructuring of mechanisms regulating commercial relations between developed and developing countries, which still remain in a poor state, but they are insufficient.

Two additional factors have caused a deterioration in the terms of trade: the first was the increase in oil prices, which brought about a direct loss of income and, at the same time, a further deterioration in the terms of trade. The industrial countries, as we have seen, were able to cover a large part of their oil import expenditures by increased exports to the oil-exporting countries. On the other hand, the Third World countries have had to bear almost all of these increased oil expenditures without being able to increase their exports to the oil-exporting countries.

The second additional factor has been the recession in the industrial countries, which has on the one hand reduced the export possibilities of the developing countries while, on the other, it increased the cost of their imports of manufactures. We should bear in mind that almost all the exports of the developing countries are directed to the industrial countries and that the volume of their exports depends mainly on effective demand in the industrial countries. This explains in large part the low level of exports from the developing countries. For example, the annual rate of growth of exports from the oil-importing developing countries dropped to 7.8 percent for the 1973-78 period as compared with 14.9 percent during the years 1970-73 and it was only 0.1 percent for the least developed countries.[8]

Public Assistance

Another factor that has contributed to the deterioration of the economic situation in the Third World countries is the reduction in public assistance from the developed countries. This assistance is now being given only at the rate of 0.35 percent of the GDP of the industrial countries, that is, at a rate half of the 0.70 percent that was established as an objective by the United Nations.

In current dollars, public assistance given by the countries of the Committee on Development Assistance of the OECD, reached $25 billion in 1981 as compared with $8.13 billion in 1970, but in relation to GDP it fell from 0.40 percent to 0.35 percent. Certain countries, including Austria, Belgium, Canada, the Netherlands, Norway, Sweden, Switzerland, and the United Kingdom increased their contribution. Others, including the United States and Japan, have considerably reduced their assistance. The Netherlands and Denmark and France are in the lead with 1.08, 0.73 and 0.71 percent respectively, which exceeds the U.N. objective. Japan's assistance is only 0.28 percent of its GDP.[9] Official development assistance, by country, as a percent of GNP is shown in Figure 4.4.

The attitude of the United States, which had formerly been more generous toward the developing countries, has become inexplicable in recent years. Its assistance, which in 1969-70 was 0.4 percent of GDP, has been reduced by one-half; now it represents no more than 0.2 percent of GDP. Thus between 1980 and 1981, there was a reduction of $1378 million.

On the other hand, an encouraging sign is that since 1975, the OPEC countries have been furnishing large amounts of assistance, about 1.44 percent of their GDP, and this has made possible an increase of almost 20 percent in assistance beyond that of the member countries of the Committee for Development Assistance (DAC).

Table 4.3 provides a synoptic comparison of the public assistance given by the main donors in 1981. As is indicated in this table:

1. The total public development assistance from all donors — CDA countries, OPEC countries, and CMEA countries — was $32 billion in 1981.

TABLE 4.3
Main Suppliers of Public Assistance in 1981:
A Synoptic Comparison

	Public Development Assistance (million dollars)	Percentage Share of GDP
United States	5,760	0.20
France	4,122	0.71
F. R. of Germany	3,182	0.46
Japan	3,353	0.20
United Kingdom	2,194	0.43
Netherlands	1,630	1.08
Canada	1,187	0.43
Sweden	916	0.83
Belgium	574	0.59
Australia	649	0.421
Denmark	405	0.73
Norway	467	0.82
Italy	670	0.12
Switzerland	236	0.24
Austria	317	0.48
Finland	135	0.28
New Zealand	67	0.29
TOTAL of CDA countries	25,461	0.35
OPEC countries	5,197*	1.44
Saudi Arabia	1,956	3.13
Kuwait	1,099	5.14
Iraq	860	2.29
United Arab Emirates	707	5.42
Qatar	251	5.60
Others	324	0.14
CMEA countries	1,852	0.11
USSR	1,432	0.14
Eastern Europe	420	0.07
TOTAL public development assistance	32,500	n.d.

*for the year 1979.

Source: OECD, *Cooperation for Development*, 1981.

FIGURE 4.4
Official Development Assistance
as a Percentage of GNP

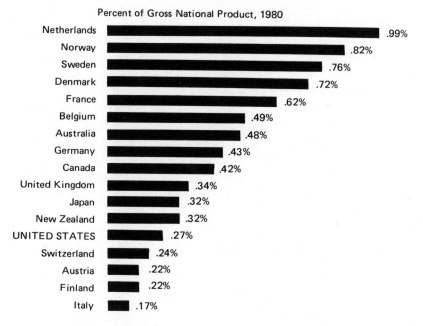

Percent of Gross National Product, 1980

Netherlands	.99%
Norway	.82%
Sweden	.76%
Denmark	.72%
France	.62%
Belgium	.49%
Australia	.48%
Germany	.43%
Canada	.42%
United Kingdom	.34%
Japan	.32%
New Zealand	.32%
UNITED STATES	.27%
Switzerland	.24%
Austria	.22%
Finland	.22%
Italy	.17%

Source: OECD, *DAC Chairman's Report*, 1981.

2. Three-quarters of this assistance was supplied by the CDA countries, 17.7 percent by the OPEC countries, and 6.3 percent by the CMEA countries.

Furthermore, it should be noted that of the total net assistance by the CDA countries, only $11.3 billion — that is, 51 percent — consisted of "gifts and contributions with a giftlike character," whereas $10.2 billion, almost the other half, represented loans and other similar types of public assistance. Therefore, the total contribution of 0.35 percent of GDP did not consist of real assistance for development in the narrower definition of this term.

THE OIL CRISIS HAS DEEPENED
THE EXTERNAL OVER-INDEBTEDNESS

To these two factors — the deterioration of the terms of trade and the reduction of public assistance — that have increased the external dependence of the non-oil exporting developing countries, must be added the burden these countries have been carrying as a result of the increase in oil prices in 1973-74 and in 1978-79.

The cost of oil, which for these countries as a whole was $8 billion in 1973, increased to $24 billion in 1974 and reached $51 billion in 1980. As a result of this increase, the ratio of their oil imports, which formerly was 13 percent of the value of their total exports, rose to 25 percent in 1980. The cost in relation to their GDP as 1.5 percent in 1973 and 5 percent in 1980.[10] This situation is likely to deteriorate further in the years to come.

These three factors have had the result of increasing the current account deficits of these countries as shown below and in Figure 4.4.

1973	$ 11.6 billion
1975	46.5
1978	39.2
1979	58.9
1980	86.2
1981	99.0
1982	97.0

The deficits differ according to the country but the countries most affected are those with small incomes.

In order to meet the deficits in their balances of payments, the non-oil developing countries have been obliged to resort to various forms of financing and especially to loans made under prevailing market conditions. Thus their external debts have mounted to a tremendous and alarming size. They rose by 20 percent a year during the 1973-80 period and reached $505 billion in 1982, as compared with $97 billion in 1973. Figure 4.5 gives the evolution of the long-term external debt of non-oil developing countries in billions of U.S. dollars between 1973 and 1982.[12]

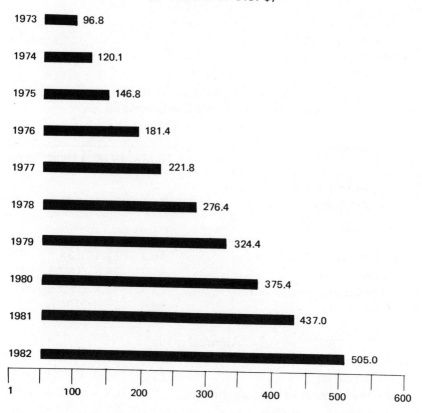

FIGURE 4.5
Long-Term External Debt of Non-Oil Developing Countries
(in billions of U.S. $)

Note: Includes public and publicly guaranteed long-term debt as well as private debt incurred without guarantee.

Source: International Monetary Fund, *World Economic Outlook*, April 1982.

Debt Distribution

The distribution of the external debt of non-oil developing countries by sources of lending, according to IMF, appears in Table 4.4.

TABLE 4.4
Non-Oil Developing Countries'
Long-Term External Debt, 1973-82
(in billions of U.S. dollars)

	1973	1978	1980	1982
Total outstanding debt of non-oil developing countries	96.8	276.4	375.4	505.2
By type of creditor				
Official creditors	48.3	117.4	155.5	199.5
Governments	35.7	79.6	102.1	128.1
International institutions	12.6	37.8	53.4	71.4
Private creditors	48.5	159.0	220.0	305.7
By analytical group				
Net oil exporters	15.6	61.4	78.0	107.0
Net oil importers	81.2	214.9	297.4	398.2
Major exporters of manufactures	38.3	108.4	143.4	194.1
Low income countries	21.6	47.3	62.3	79.7
Other net oil importers	21.3	59.2	91.7	124.3
By area				
Africa	13.1	38.7	49.2	66.0
Asia	27.0	62.9	85.6	121.4
Europe	11.6	33.5	54.2	67.2
Middle East	8.5	24.6	32.9	41.3
Western Hemisphere	36.6	116.7	153.4	209.3

Source: I.M.F., *World Economic Outlook*, 1982, p. 170.

The table shows that the largest part of the debt derives from different sources of private lending that amounted to a total of $305 billion at the end of 1982. The recourse to the international capital market is made under less favorable conditions than for the public debt, and this creates supplementary burdens for these countries.[13]

The private banks are playing a progressively larger role in the financing of the non-oil developing countries. At the end of 1982, the largest debt the non-oil developing countries had was that to the banks, which represented 72 percent of the total foreign debt of these countries (see Table 4.5). The total of non-oil developing countries was estimated by the International Monetary Fund at $505.2 billion at the end of 1982. Of this debt, $199.5 billion represents official debt and $305.7 billion the private debt.

TABLE 4.5
Major Debtors Among Non-Oil Developing Countries

Countries	Total debt*	Bank debt*
Mexico	71.3	56.9
Brasil	69.6	52.7
Argentina	35.7	24.8
Korea	32.8	19.9
South Africa	11.2	11.2
Yugoslavia	19.7	10.7
Chile	14.5	10.5
Philippines	10.2	10.2
Greece	10.0	9.8
Hungary	8.6	7.7
Portugal	10.0	7.5
Israel	18.3	6.0
Colombia	5.4	5.4
Romania	10.5	5.1
Thailand	8.1	5.1
TOTAL	335.9	243.5

*In billions of U.S. dollars.

Source: Bank for International Settlements and IMF estimates.

SEVENTY-TWO PERCENT OF NEW LOANS
GO FOR DEBT SERVICE PAYMENTS

The most disturbing feature of the economic situation of the non-oil developing countries is the enormous amount of external debt service payments required annually from these countries. The servicing payments due (interest plus amortization) increased from $10.9 billion in 1971 to $110 billion in 1981 or to an average annual rate of 26 percent. In fact, the percent increase in service payments has surpassed the increase in the amount of the total debt (the former increased 5 times as compared with the latter which increased only by 3.8 times). This difference is a result of the worsening conditions in the capital markets, which have become in recent years progressively more unfavorable for borrowers. Thus, the relationship between the total amount of debt in relation to the service payments, which at the beginning of 1970 was 12.5 percent, increased to 20 percent in 1982. This relationship will deteriorate still further to the detriment of the debtor countries if interest rates continue to remain high. In the period 1972-81, the average financial cost of the debt contracted at floating rates, which consti-tute the majority of developing country's debts, increased from 7.9 percent to 18 percent. According to a statement by the managing director of the IMF, "for every one percent increase in world interest rates, some $2 billion is added to their debt service costs."[14]

Amortization Absorbs 62 Percent of Debt Service

The main factor that accounts for the rapid increase in debt service payments is the length of maturity of the loans, which averages in most cases from 8 to 9 years and therefore requires a rapid amortization. The composition of the service payments due in 1982 alone on the outstanding total debt of $505 billion was:

Interest	$ 40.8 billion
Amortization	$ 67.0 billion
TOTAL	$ 107.8 billion

Thus, in the year 1982, repayment of principal was 62 percent of the total. For the entire period 1975 to 1982, amortization accounted for 62.5 percent while interest represented 37.5 percent.[15]

Of all types of foreign debts, private loans bear the most adverse terms for the developing countries, as shown in Table 4.6.

From the statistics shown in Table 4.5, it appears that total export credits and other private financing (last two items in the table) amount to $368 billion, with an annual servicing of $100.8 billion, corresponding to 70 percent of the entire debt. Generally, CDA loans are on average at 2.6 percent interest and 31 years maturity, including a grace period of 9 years; Development Assitance Committee (DAC) export credits are on average at 7-8 percent interest and around 8 years maturity; Euro-lending in recent years has been at about 18 percent interest and about 7 years maturity.[16]

A Paradoxical Phenomenon

How do developing countries manage to pay this enormous amount for the servicing of their debts? By obtaining new loans every year.

TABLE 4.6
Distribution, According to the Nature of Loans, of the Total Debt of the Developing Countries and Servicing Charges for 1981
(in billions of dollars)

	Debt	Debt Servicing %
CDA bilateral and multilateral	118.0	5.9
Other multilateral financing	38.0	5.0
Export credits	148.0	41.9
Other financing at market rates	220.0	58.9
TOTAL	524.0	111.7

Source: OECD, Financing Problems of Non-Oil Developing Countries, p. 19.

But what is bound to prove eventually destabilizing is that the amount that developing countries pay every year for the servicing of their debts alone absorbs 72 percent of all new loans made, as shown in Table 4.7.

It can be stated therefore that, for the period in question, the aggregate payments for debt service plus repayments of principal have been 72 percent of the total amounts of new loans granted.

In the final analysis, the international financial mechanism operates in a vicious circle because less-developed countries are trapped in a situation of having to borrow increasing amounts in order to meet their needs. This situation is the consequence of the repayment period of these loans, which only averages a short seven to eight years. Were such repayment periods to be negotiated on a long-term basis, this destabilizing vicious circle would be stopped. This point is elaborated in Chapter 8.

TABLE 4.7
Debt Servicing and New Loans for Developing Countries, 1974-82
(in billions of dollars)

Year	Debt service payments	New Loans, Net (after repayment of principal)
1975	26.2	35.0
1976	32.2	37.8
1977	41.0	47.8
1978	56.9	72.0
1979	73.6	61.0
1980	91.2	58.6
1981	111.7	67.8
Cumulative total	432.8	380.0
Cumulative repayments of principal between 1974 & 1980		218.0
TOTAL of new loans		598.0

Source: OECD data, *L'Endettement Extérieur* (Paris, 1981), pp. 17-18.

NOTES

1. A very interesting and well-documented analysis of North-South problems may be found in the *Report of the Willy Brandt Commission*, a document of historic significance that also opens new paths for a changed international economic policy. This report has been commented upon by eminent personalities. See *Towards One World? International Responses to the Brandt Report*, edited by the Friedrich Ebert Foundation (London, 1981); see also *Global Strategy for Growth, A Report on North-South Issues*, by a study group under the chairmanship of Lord McFadzean of Kelvinsire (London: Trade Policy Research Center, 1981). More recently: *Common Crisis North-South* — Cooperation for World Recovery — The Brandt Commission (London: Pan Books, 1983).

2. *Report of the Willy Brandt Commission*, p. 53.

3. The developing countries are divided into two groups — "oil-exporting countries," and "non-oil-exporting countries." The "oil-exporting countries" are the following twelve:

Algeria	Kuwait	Qatar
Indonesia	Libya	Saudi Arabia
Iraq	Nigeria	United Arab Emirates
Iran	Oman	Venezuela

In the category of non-oil-exporting developing countries are included all the other Third World countries. However, this category includes some countries that are not oil exporters, but whose economic situation, terms of trade and external payments are somewhat different from the main oil-exporting countries because their exports do not cover more than two-thirds of their imports. This means that they do not have a surplus. Among these countries are: Bahrein, Bolivia, Congo, Egypt, Malaysia, Mexico, Syria, and Tunisia.

More details of the classification of countries are given in IMF, *World Economic Outlook*, 1982, p. 140.

4. World Bank, *1981 Atlas* (Washington, D.C., 1982).

5. According to the World Bank, *World Development Report*, (1980), income (GDP) per capita in billions of dollars in 1980 was:

Industrial countries	9664
Intermediate countries	1520
Low income countries	245

6. The bibliography on the problem of poverty is extensive; among recent works on the subject see: Peter Townsend, *The Concept of Poverty* (London: Heinemann, 1970); John Kenneth Galbraith, *The Nature of Mass Poverty* (Cambridge, Mass.: Harvard University Press, 1979); Susan MacGregor, *The Politics of Poverty* (London: Longman, 1981); David Dennison, *The Politics of Poverty* (London: Probeston, 1981); A. Tevrédjze, *La Pauvreté Richesse*

des Peuples (Paris: Editions ouvrières, 1978).

7. See also, GATT, *International Trade in 1981 and present Prospects*, (Geneva, 1982); A. I. Yeats, *Trade and Development Politics* (London: McMillan, 1981); C. P Kindleberger, "Less Developed Countries and the International Capital Markets," in *International Money*, 1981.

8. OECD, *Cooperation for Development*, 1980, p. 88.

9. OECD, *Cooperation for Development*, 1980, p. 112.

10. OECD, *Financing Problems of Non-Oil Developing Countries*, March, 1980.

11. IMF, *World Economic Outlook*, 1982, p. 158.

12. Ibid., p. 170. Estimates of the foreign debt of developing countries are made by various international organizations, in particular IMF, World Bank, and OECD. The figures contained in OECD, *External Debit of Developing Countries* (Paris, 1981) are higher than those of the IMF. The difference is $87 billion for the year 1981 alone ($524 billion in the latter compared with $437 billion in the former). This difference results because OECD statistics include a greater number of developing countries than the IMF statistics. In this study, data on debt derive mainly from the IMF sources.

13. According to the World Bank, the public debt interest rate averaged 7.8 percent for 1978, with a 16-year maturity and a grace period of 4.4 years. On the other hand, the interest rate for the private debt averaged 13.64 percent and the maturity 8.7 years. In 1979-82, the terms are even less favorable, as the interest rate has reached around 18-20 percent, as contrasted with a rate of 10-12 percent for 1983.

14. Address by J. de Larosière, managing director of the International Monetary Fund before the Economic and Social Council of the United Nations, July 13, 1982, Geneva.

15. OECD figures (in billions of $) are as follows:

	Interest	*Amortization*	*Total*
1975	9.5	16.7	26.2
1976	11.8	20.4	32.2
1977	14.3	26.7	41.0
1978	19.8	37.1	56.9
1979	26.0	47.6	73.6
1980	34.9	56.3	91.2
1981	46.5	65.2	111.7
TOTALS	162.8	270.0	432.8

16. OECD, *Financing Problems of Non-oil Developing Countries*, p. 5.

5

THE ENERGY CRISIS AND
THE PROBLEM OF OIL

ENERGY, A MAIN FACTOR IN ECONOMIC GROWTH

To understand properly the extent of the influence of the energy factor on economic growth, it is necessary to be aware of the degree to which, in any country, economic progress and standards of living depend on the energy used. It is this factor which, together with the technological factor, plays a key role in the increase of national income. Statistics show a particularly close relationship between energy use and national income. During the 13-year period between 1960 and 1973, the increase of energy supplies averaged 5 percent annually in the industrialized countries, which corresponded to an average annual economic growth of 5 percent in these countries.

In the years of the 1950s and the 1960s, especially, the production of several energy sources showed extraordinary increases. The production of primary energy of all types grew about 3.3 times, from 2.7 billion tons in 1950 to 9 billion in 1975. This increase in energy production reflected in great part a large growth in oil and gas production. At present, these two products account for almost 70 percent of world energy consumption. In particular, the consumption of oil tripled between 1950 and 1975 so that by 1980 it constituted 50 percent of the energy consumed in the world (52 percent in Western Europe, 44 percent in the United States and 49 percent in the OECD countries as a whole).[1]

The energy factor, furthermore, helps to explain the large gap between the rich and poor countries. In the rich countries the consumption of energy per capita is 100 times more than in the poor countries. Even in the industrial countries there is a difference in energy consumption reflecting mainly the degree of development of each country. For example, an American uses as much commercial energy as 2 Germans or 3 Japanese or 6 Yugoslavs or 53 Indians or Indonesians.

However, the successive increases in the prices of crude oil since 1973 have fundamentally changed the relationship between production and energy use and have had unfavorable effects on national incomes. These changes have in turn accentuated the fragility of the world economy. Thus, the very low level of energy used during the period 1975-80 as compared with the past was accompanied by a progressive reduction in economic growth, which averaged only about 1 to 2 percent annually. The decline in oil deliveries from Iran at the end of 1978 and the large fall in oil production as a result of the war between Iran and Iraq further intensified tensions on the world oil market and resulted in new price increases as well as a reduction in oil consumption.

By early 1981 oil prices had risen about 170 percent from their late 1978 level.

While the oil price increases in 1973 were imposed on an economy that was just beginning to slow down after a strong and synchronized boom with capacity utilization at record levels, the 1979 oil price rises occurred at a time when economic activity in the OECD area was in a low-growth period. The unprecedented economic boom in 1972-73 had led to a surge in commodity prices just prior to the shock of the first oil price increase. By contrast, in 1978, commodity prices had not risen as much, and unit labor costs were growing only slightly. The slowdown of economic activity in the OECD economies in 1980-81 may in fact be attributed to a large extent to the direct and indirect effects of the shock of the second oil price increase.

The full impact of the second oil price increase on inflation, output, and productivity has still to work itself out. The estimated growth of real GDP in the OECD countries has dropped by some

2.5 percentage points below the 1977-79 level. Estimates by the International Energy Agency have indicated that GNP in 1981 in its member countries may very well be 6 percentage points (some $500 billion) lower than it might have been without the oil price increases. In addition, the cumulative loss of real income to OPEC countries, due to their terms-of-trade deterioration, amounted to over 4 percent by the end of 1981. The combined output and terms-of-trade loss will thus accumulate to represent over 10 percent of the GNP of these two areas or close to $900 billion in 1981 prices. Furthermore, the induced tightening of monetary and fiscal policies, in reaction to the inflationary effect of oil price increases, has been responsible for a further reduction in demand, thereby bringing the total loss of real income resulting from the higher oil prices of 1979-80, in the OECD area alone, to an amount which may be estimated at more than one trillion dollars in 1981.

The industrialized countries are likely to undergo even greater constraints, during the period to 1985, that will have economic repercussions on their economic structures in the medium-term. Of particular importance will be the induced effects of transformations in the ranking of economic policy goals by the governments of the industrial countries, as one government after another begins to rank the objective of attaining full employment and full-employment-related growth below the objective of combating inflation through a reduction in aggregate demand. But if inflations are, even only in part, oil-induced and therefore imported and if the measures taken to combat inflation are government imposed and therefore domestic in nature (for example the reduction in aggregate demand) a serious asymmetry in policies may develop in the future, as it did twice in the recent past, unless the price strategies of the oil producers are brought into line with the economic strategies of the oil consumers; or unless a degree of sufficient independence is gained by the latter group of countries with respect to their energy requirements so as to enable them to avoid the consequences of further potential oil price increases.

Energy Demand and Energy Dependence

We shall now examine the progress that has been made since 1973 in reducing the dependence on oil imports and the effects of oil price increases on the world economy.

The reduction of total primary energy consumption per unit of GDP, from 100 in 1973 to 87.3 in 1980, to a level lower than it was even in 1960, merits special attention. Between 1960 and 1973, the energy coefficient (percent change in energy over percent change in GDP) for the OECD region as a whole was unity. During the period 1973-80, on the other hand, the value of the energy coefficient fell from unity to a mere 0.2, as shown in Table 5.1.

This drastic decline in energy-production requirements reflects price-induced structural changes in the use of energy in the OECD economies, but it also reflects the consequences of sluggish economic activity that has impacted disproportionately on energy-intensive industries (steel, cement, shipbuilding, automobiles). To a large extent, energy-saving structural changes have been price-induced.[2] The result of these changes is that, between 1973 and 1980, the Gross Domestic Product (GDP) has increased in the OECD countries by 19 percent, but the energy consumption had grown by only 4 percent and oil use was even 3 percent below the 1973 level.[3] Thus the energy policy adopted after 1973 has generated gains both in energy efficiency and in the substitution of other fuels for oil.

TABLE 5.1
Relations Between Output, Energy, and Oil Prices
1960-80, in OECD Countries

	1960-73	1973-80
Real GDP, (annual % change)	5.0	2.5
Real oil price (annual % change)	−2.0	22.5
Total primary energy (annual % change)	5.2	0.5
Total primary energy/GDP ((3)÷(1))	1.04	0.2
Annual % change in the ratio of		
total primary energy to GDP	0.2	−1.9

Source: Compiled by the author.

By contrast to the experience of the OECD countries, the growth of energy consumption by LDCs remained close to historical rates (above 5 percent annually). This has serious implications not only for the ability of LDCs to finance their future energy requirements and shifts to energy-saving capital, but also for the oil-pricing policies of the producing countries.

THE EFFECTS OF OIL PRICE INCREASES
ON THE WORLD ECONOMY

As we have pointed out in the analysis contained in our earlier book,[4] the sharp increase in oil prices since January 1974 contributed to an acceleration of the recession, but was not its only cause. The increase in fact revealed the structural weaknesses of the economic system and reinforced the influence of many factors that had already begun to provoke latent inflationary effects.

At the beginning of the 1970s the world economy had already experienced economic difficulties as a result especially of the appearance of inflationary pressures in several countries; the monetary system was shaken by the abandonment of the link between the dollar and the gold-exchange-standard (August 1971) as well as by the ending of fixed exchange rates at the beginning of 1973. The quadrupling of oil prices at the end of 1973 only accelerated the recessionary trend that had already made its appearance. It may be noted that on the eve of the oil crisis, industrial production had registered a great decline of up to 13 percent, while the increase of consumers' prices was 10 percent in 1973 and monetary policy as well as budgetary policy was directed toward measures restricting economic activity.[5]

In addition, it must be recognized that one of the causes of this sharp increase in oil prices was the lack of price adjustment for this product in the market during a long period of time. History shows that if the adjustment of relative prices for a product is delayed over a very long period and does not reflect general market conditions, there will be, at some time or other, an abrupt rise in the price of the product. The effects will be all the more serious if the product's role in the economy is a predominant one. This has been true with respect to two basic products, oil and gold, that play a major role in the functioning of the economic and monetary systems. The events of the Yom Kippur War served as a pretext of a political nature for a sharp increase in oil prices.

Gold prices followed a similar pattern. The price of gold was maintained stable for more than 35 years, as a result of international agreement. Had the signatory states decided to readjust the price in relation to the prices of other goods during the decade of the 1960s, monetary policy would have been different and would not have had the same repercussions on present-day economic life.

On the other hand, this policy of maintaining oil prices at a very low level discouraged the search for other sources of energy, encouraged waste, and provoked strong reactions on the part of the producing countries. In fact, the price of oil not only remained unchanged over a long period but it even dropped as a result of the unilateral decisions of the large international oil companies, decisions that were taken without consulting the producing countries. Thus, the price of oil fell by 8.7 percent in February 1959 and a further 6 percent in August 1960. These decisions led to the creation in September 1960 by the leaders of the five most important oil exporting countries – Saudi Arabia, Iran, Iraq, Kuwait, and Venezuela – of the Organization of Oil Exporting Countries (OPEC) with the aim of studying a system which would ensure price stability and would take into consideration the interests of producers and consumers.

The Absence of an Agreement

During the period 1960-70, the exporting countries sought unsuccessfully to obtain an increase in oil prices from the large oil companies. Despite their repeated demands, especially after the institution of the floating rate for the dollar on August 15, 1971 and its first devaluation of 8 percent, OPEC was confronted with a negative attitude. It was only in October 1978 after several days of fruitless discussion in Vienna during the Yom Kippur War that OPEC decided to unilaterally increase the price of crude oil, which in three months almost quadrupled, rising from $3.01 to $11.63 a barrel.

Only then did the oil exporting countries acquire virtual control of their wealth.[6] It must indeed be recognized that the blame for the economic and monetary disorder created as a result of the uncontrolled prices of oil must be attributed in large part to the industrial countries that sought to profit from their international economic and political strength.

The worst result of the oil policy of the industrial oil-consuming countries was that these countries did not take advantage of this experience and adopt a new and appropriate policy aimed at avoiding a repetition of their mistake. After the increase of oil prices in 1973-74, an increase larger than that in the price index in general, the industrial countries and especially those with strong currencies wished to profit from the devaluation of the dollar that took place during the 1975-78 period.

In fact, the price of oil in dollars was held at a stable level between 1974 and 1978, but in real terms the price dropped. In this connection, the data presented by a Working Party of the OECD and presented in Figure 5.1 are very interesting. The following conclusions may be drawn from Figure 5.1:

1. The real prices of energy for final users (residential, commercial, industrial, and transport) dropped in the 1960s and this decline continued until 1973.

2. As a result of the events of 1973-74 oil prices showed an abrupt inverse upward movement.

3. During the 1975-78 period, real prices fell again before resuming their increase in 1979.

Thus, the real price of crude oil remained more or less constant from February 1974 to July 1979. In June 1979 the real price of crude oil was 10 percent less than the highest price registered in 1974.[7]

It is true that price fluctuations differed from country to country. Whereas a sharp drop was observed in most of the European countries and Japan, prices dropped only slightly in the United States and Canada because of governmental measures aimed at protecting oil of domestic origin from foreign competition.

The fall in the real price of oil between 1975 and 1980 is due to the devaluation of the dollar. During all this period the dollar

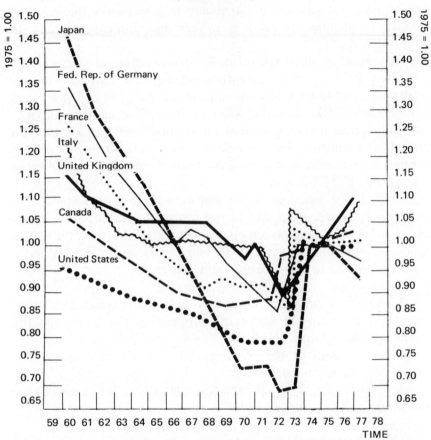

FIGURE 5.1
Energy Prices to Final Users
(1975 = 100)

Note: This is an index of combined energy prices to final users consisting of: energy component of consumer price index (excluding gasoline) divided by the total index of consumer prices; energy component of wholesale price index divided by a composite of prices for labor and capital; and gasoline prices divided by total index of consumer prices. Each component was weighted by its respective share in total final energy demand.

Source: OECD, Working Party *No. 4*, 1980.

continued its devaluation in relation to such other strong currencies as the Swiss franc, the mark, the yen, the pound sterling, the French franc, and other currencies.[8]

Thus, the industrialized countries, with the exception of the United States, instead of seeking to reach an agreement with oil exporters for annual readjustments of prices, endeavored to profit from the devaluation of the dollar in order to reduce their oil-payments burden. Such an attitude could only provoke a reaction on the part of the OPEC countries.

I recall what the Minister of Oil of Saudi Arabia, Sheik Yamani, told me in a conversation I had with him in Riyadh in February 1977: "Notice," he said, "how the industrialized countries exploit us by taking advantage of the devaluation of the dollar." He added: "The day will not be long in coming when certain countries will react forcefully to combat this attitude and such a reaction will provoke a new and large increase in oil prices." He was right. One year later, in spite of the opposition of Sheik Yamani, the OPEC countries decided upon successive increases in oil prices, so that by the beginning of 1980 there was a rise of 130 percent as compared with the 1978 price. At the end of 1980, prices increased again by 10 percent, resulting in a rise of 20 times since 1959. In fact, the price of Arabian light crude, which was $1.80 a barrel in 1959, reached a price of almost $34.00 a barrel at the end of 1982. The evolution of the price of crude oil per barrel since 1973 has been the following:

1959	$ 1.80
1973	$ 4.18
1974	$11.35
1980	$32.81
1981	$37.25
1982	$34.30
1983 (May)	$29.00

As there is still no long-term agreement between the oil-producing and oil-consuming countries that would provide for an annual readjustment of oil prices and take into account various relevant factors, it will be impossible in the future to avoid fluctuations harmful to economic growth.

The Western world has in the past preferred instead to remain inactive, though confronted with a problem of primary importance to it, thus giving to the extremists in the oil-exporting countries reasons for the adoption of a policy of successive and uncontrolled increases in oil-prices. At the same time, the Western world has given the oil price increases more importance than the problem of developing new, more effective and more rational policies that would deal with the problem of the structural weaknesses in their economies.

Oil As a Fiscal Instrument

Another factor that has aggravated the oil crisis is the use of petroleum and its derivatives as a fiscal instrument in the industrial countries.

In fact, the taxes applied to gasoline products have been, in many countries, two and even three times the initial cost of the oil used. Table 5.2 gives the percentage rates for taxes on gasoline as compared with the cost of oil before taxes in 1970, 1973, and 1979.[9]

It may be noted that in the United States, the tax proportion is minimal as compared with that in the European countries. In 1970

TABLE 5.2
Taxes on Gasoline as a Percentage of Cost of Oil

	1970	1973	1979
Fed. Rep. of Germany	264	239	126
France	290	234	180
Italy	364	335	209
United Kingdom	257	160	47
Japan	142	100	72
United States	44	38	18
Canada	–	71	48
Average	–	168	100

Source: World Bank: World Development Report, 1980.

Italy was in the lead with a tax 3.6 times higher than the initial cost, while the countries in which the tax rates have been lowest are the United States, the United Kingdom, and Japan.

Thus, the governments of the continental European countries have sought to make an impact on consumers not only through increases in oil product prices but also to benefit from the surtax that brings them large fiscal revenues.[10]

In many countries, it was not, therefore, the purchase price of crude oil that brought about increases in costs of production in general and adverse effects on consumers, but rather the final price of oil products, including taxes. However, while oil taxation is unavoidable (if it were not applied, governments would have to replace it by other fiscal measures if only in order to fill the gap that would thereby be created in their budgets), the IMF, noting that the effective rates of taxes on gasoline had greatly diminished since 1973, has concluded that "a re-evaluation of these rates is required."[11]

Beneficial Effects on Industrial Countries

Although, as we have stated earlier, the effects of the increase in oil prices were less than had been forecast, there is no doubt that this increase stimulated the acceleration of inflation in most countries.[12] Nevertheless, the increases in oil prices, which have resulted in an enormous movement of capital from the oil-consuming countries to the oil-producing countries during the 1974-79 period, may be said to have had beneficial effects on the economies of the industrial countries. Why is this so? Because a large part of the funds transferred to the oil-producing countries were returned to the industrial countries in the form of purchases of capital goods and services that permitted the industrial countries to maintain and strengthen their economies and to prevent a rapid acceleration of the recession.

Indeed, this is a demonstration of the fact that a redistribution of world income can have favorable effects on the world economy as a whole. The balance of payments surpluses of the OPEC countries fell from $70 billion in 1974 to only $3 billion in 1978, particularly as a result of their increase in imports of goods and services, and to $25 billion in 1982. For 1978, the total exports from the industrial countries to the OPEC countries reached $100 billion, an amount that covered 76 percent of the expenditures in that year for the purchase of oil. During the entire 1974-82 period the oil-producing countries received $1680 billion and spent on their imports $894 billion, that is 53 percent of the amount they received, and 62 percent for the period 1978-82.[13]

Table 5.3 shows the evolution of the current account of oil-exporting countries during the period 1973-82.

The Oil Exporting Countries: an Important Economic Factor

According to the estimates of the IMF,[14] the total current account surplus available for disposition for the period 1974-81 by exporting countries amounted to $475 billion, the disposition of which was as follows:

Fund and World Bank	$ 11 billion
Loans and grants to non-oil developing countries	$ 62 billion
Bank deposits in industrial countries (including Euro-currency deposits)	$160 billion
Other placements*	$242 billion
	$475 billion

*Includes net acquisitions of governments securities, corporate stocks and bonds, bilateral lending (namely to governments), real estate, and other direct investments.

During the decade of the 1980s, the amount of the "surplus" will depend on the evolution of the price of oil.

The fact is that 12 oil-exporting countries[15] constitute an economic factor and have a privileged situation. The 12 countries together amounted for some 15 percent of world exports in 1980, about 7 percent of world imports, 6 percent of world GDP, and 44 percent of global oil production.

So, by controlling not only the supply of oil but also the movement of capital, "these countries hold in their hand the economic

TABLE 5.3
Oil-Exporting Countries:
Summary of Current Account
(in billions of U.S. dollars)

	1973	1974	1976	1979	1980	1982
Oil exports (F.O.B.)	39.0	117.9	133.2	214.0	297.4	244.0
Imports (F.O.B.)	−20.2	−35.8	−68.1	−100.8	−130.3	−165.8
Balance on merchandise trade	18.8	82.2	65.1	113.2	167.1	78.2
Net services and private transfers	−12.2	−13.9	-24.8	-43.4	−52.1	−53.2
Balance on current account	6.7	68.3	40.3	69.8	115.0	25.0

Source: I.M.F., *World Economic Outlook*, 1982, p. 160.

and political future of the world," as the American magazine *Business Week* has pointed out.[16]

WORLD ENERGY OUTLOOK

The energy problem is, in fact, more serious than is generally believed. The provisional slackening in the market can create some disillusions, but, as the International Energy Agency remarks in its recent survey, "the current outlook for short-term stability in energy markets and the oil market in particular is deceptive because signals in today's surplus oil market do not reflect the underlying medium and long-term trends."[17] And, as the Agency adds, "the demand restraining effects of earlier oil price rises will tend to be gradually absorbed over time." The same attitude was adopted during the Meeting of Governing Board at Ministerial Level of May 24, 1982. In their communiqué, they said:

> Ministers welcomed the reduced current demand for oil and noted the resulting weakening of oil prices. However, they recognised that there could be a turnaround in overall demand on short notice when the existing drawdown of oil stocks ends or if a strong upturn in economic activity occurs and the risk of a price shock caused by political disturbances remains.[18]

World Production of Oil

Indeed the supply-demand situation for oil at the beginning of the decade of the 1980s will be influenced by the tensions on the world market and by the demands of the importing countries. The world oil production, which was 65.3 million barrels daily in 1979, declined to 57.9 million barrels in 1982, an amount equal to the production of the year 1973 (57.9 to 58.3 million barrels daily).

Table 5.4 shows the evolution of world production of crude oil between 1973, 1979, and 1982.

TABLE 5.4
World Crude Oil Production
(in millions of barrels a day)

	1973	1979	1981	1982
Oil exporting countries	31.1	31.3	23.3	19.6
Saudi Arabia	7.6	9.5	9.8	6.5
Kuwait	3.0	2.5	1.1	0.8
United Arab Emirates	1.5	1.8	1.5	1.3
Libyan Arab Jamahiriya	2.2	2.1	1.1	1.2
Iraq	2.0	3.5	1.0	0.9
Iran	5.9	3.1	1.3	2.0
Venezuela	3.4	2.4	2.1	1.9
Nigeria	2.0	2.3	1.4	1.3
Algeria	1.1	1.1	0.8	0.9
Indonesia	1.3	1.6	1.6	1.3
Mexico	0.5	1.6	2.6	3.0
Egypt	0.2	0.5	0.6	0.7
Industrial countries	13.8	14.7	14.8	15.1
United States	11.0	10.2	10.2	10.2
United Kingdom	—*	1.6	1.8	2.1
Nonmember countries	9.1	12.3	12.6	12.7
USSR	8.6	11.8	12.2	12.3
China, People's Republic of	1.1	2.1	2.0	2.0
Others				
TOTAL	58.3	65.6	59.1	56.5

*Production in the United Kingdom commenced in 1979.

Source: I.M.F., *World Economic Outlook*, 1982 and 1983, p. 206 and p. 237.

Distribution of Oil Reserves

In the long term, the oil problem is likely to remain acute. As mentioned earlier, this energy source at present meets about 50 percent of the total world needs for energy, but it is not inexhaustible. Although estimates differ, it appears that known oil reserves will not allow the maintenance of present-day production for more than 30 or 40 years, and present production is relatively low. As may be seen in Table 5.5, the largest portion of these reserves — 53 percent of the total — is situated in the Middle East and this oil is of vital economic importance for the Western industrialized countries. Outside of the Soviet Union and Eastern Europe, the OPEC countries control 70 percent of the world's reserves and 50 percent of world production. The United States, including Alaska, has 15 percent of the reserves, Africa 16 percent, the Soviet Union and the Eastern countries 15 percent, and Western Europe only 2 percent.

Oil not only still remains the dominant fuel but its contribution to the overall energy needs of the OECD countries is more than twice the contribution of the second largest fuel, coal. As shown in Table 5.6, the contribution of coal is still higher in the European countries of the OECD than elsewhere. It may be noted that after 30 years of technical and commercial development, the share of nuclear energy is still below 4 percent of the total energy requirements of the OECD countries.

The discovery of new oil resources is in rapid decline as compared with the past. In fact, during the decades of the 1950s and 1960s, the expansion of oil production was stimulated by an abundance of discoveries that each year were, on the average, about six times greater than the tonnage consumed. Almost all of the petroleum resources at present known in the Middle East, in North Africa (Libya, Algeria), Nigeria, and Siberia were discovered between 1938 and 1968. On the other hand, during the 1971-78 period the discoveries represented only one-half of consumption. Between now and the year 2000, in spite of the pace of prospecting under way throughout the world, it would not appear that the amounts of oil that may be discovered can appreciably modify the estimates made until now. Undoubtedly, there do exist additional oil and hydrocarbon supply sources, both in the industrialized countries and in

TABLE 5.5
Geopolitical Distribution of Proved Oil Reserves
(January 1, 1981)
(Million metric tons)

		Percent of Total
OECD	7,977	(9.0)
OPEC	59,257	(67.0)
CPEs[a]	11,774	(13.3)
LDCs[b]	9,467	(10.7)
TOTAL World	88,475	(100.0)

[a]Centrally planned economies.
[b]Less developed countries.

Source: International Energy Agency, *Energy Outlook* (Paris, 1982).

TABLE 5.6
Regional Distribution of OECD 1980 Energy Requirements,
by Fuel
(percent)

	North America	Europe	Pacific	OECD Total
Oil	43.6	52.5	61.7	48.9
Gas	25.6	14.4	7.1	19.5
Coal	20.8	22.1	20.6	21.2
Nuclear	3.6	3.9	4.2	3.8
Others	6.4	7.1	6.4	6.6
TOTAL	100.0	100.0	100.0	100.0

Source: International Energy Agency, *Energy Outlook* (Paris, 1982).

the Third World countries. Besides the oil and gas of the North Sea, whose production has increased in recent years,[19] there have been — for example — important discoveries in Mexico during the past few years.[20]

But, the two basic characteristics of the present oil situation are, on the one hand, a tendency for production to reach a peak at today's levels and, on the other, for oil prices to be established in a unilateral way by the oil-producing countries.

This situation can be explained on economic, political, and technical grounds. First of all, the change in the structure of production and the functioning of the market that has taken place since 1974 must be taken into account. Since that time, control over production as passed from the international companies to the producing countries, which in 1980 determined output levels for 76 percent of the world's supplies as contrasted with 43 percent in 1973. They also took over the entire management of the oil resources in their territories. This change allowed the OPEC governments to sell a large part of their exports directly to the importing states and thus reduced the access to and the role of the international companies in the oil markets of the world.

In this way, the oil-exporting countries are now able to largely determine the volume of their production and the price levels for their oil products. Conscious as they are of an eventual exhaustion of their resources, they prefer to keep this national wealth intact for as long a period as possible and thus safeguard the large profits they can derive from it. Furthermore, faced with the acceleration of international inflation, they appear to be particularly concerned with the need to find all appropriate ways of maintaining the purchasing power of the capital they earn in exchange for their oil. For this reason the problem of the stability of the dollar becomes of special importance, as does the problem of maintaining the value of their financial assets over the long term; these problems are, in fact, permanent business cycle factors in the international payments system.

Because of this climate of uncertainty, the countries that are able to satisfy their needs for imports by using their oil resources prefer, as we have pointed out, to conserve their precious wealth in the soil rather than to extract it beyond their requirements. Already, several of these countries have announced that they intend to reduce production in order to protect their resources. Thus, the production of oil during the decade of the 1980s will depend on endogenous factors prevailing in the producing countries.

Are there conditions in existence that could modify this attitude of the producing countries and lead them to change their long-term policies? Only the existence of prospects for the exploitation of a large new source of energy would oblige these countries to increase their production in a significant way and to reach an agreement to this end with the importing countries.

In the absence of such an agreement — and we shall return to this point later — the oil-producing countries alone remain, in the last analysis, masters of the situation determining the volume of production and sales prices for their oil.

Furthermore, the fact that oil has no foreseeable substitute for the next two decades reinforces this position. Prices, which are in fact totally independent of production costs, will therefore depend on the decision of the producing countries alone. Undoubtedly, demand by the importing countries will play a certain role, but this is not the decisive factor. Indeed, oil will for a long time continue to be a colossal financial resource for the exporting countries because its production cost is in reality very small. In the Middle East, the extraction of a barrel of oil costs between 25 cents and 1 dollar; in the African countries it is a little higher.[21]

PROSPECTS FOR THE COMING DECADES

What are the industrialized countries doing in the face of this situation? What are they doing to develop techniques that would make possible the exploitation of new sources of energy that are so necessary to overcome the oil crisis? Are they aware of the fact that the future of their economies depends on the way in which the energy problem will be solved?

The deficit in energy supplies during the next decade will be very serious both for the industrialized countries and the oil-importing developing countries. Table 5.7, based on estimates made by the World Bank, gives us an idea of the gap between production and consumption between 1980 and 1990 for each group of countries.

TABLE 5.7
Production and Consumption of Primary Commercial Energy, 1980 and 1990
(millions of barrels daily in oil equivalent)

	1980		1990	
	Production	Consumption	Production	Consumption
Industrialized countries	50.1	70.1	72.5	92.5
Oil-importing developing countries	8.5	14.1	18.5	26.0
Planned economy countries	44.8	42.5	65.0	64.3
Oil-exporting countries	21.4	1.9	26.1	3.9

Source: World Bank, *World Development Report*, 1980, p. 117.

On the basis of this estimate, it would appear that:

1. The gap between production and consumption of primary energy — assuming the high growth rate hypothesis for the decade of the 1980s established by the World Bank — would be by 1990 comparable to that of 1980 in absolute figures for the industrialized countries, that is, 20 million barrels of oil equivalent daily. This is a large deficit. However, the percentage dependent on external sources would be reduced, from 30 percent to about 22 percent.

2. For the oil-importing developing countries, the gap would be in volume terms almost the same.

3. Only the countries of the socialist planned economies group would be in a position to have energy available in quantities sufficient to cover their needs.

4. The production surplus in the oil-exporting countries would appear to be slightly higher than the surplus in 1980 (22.2 as against 19.5 million barrels a day) but this would be less than in 1977 when it was 23.6 million barrels a day.

The Forecast of International Energy Agency

The International Energy Agency in its publication *World Energy Outlook*[22] has elaborated two assumed scenarios for price and economic growth, and has prepared an energy demand model that holds primary energy demand curves for the two scenarios that accelerate from 0.6-0.8 percent per year in the first half of the 1980s to as much as 1.7-2.6 percent per year during the 1990s.

The world oil supply is projected to remain at around 50 million barrels per day, reaching at best 53 million barrels per day by the end of the century. The results of these projections are presented in Table 5.8.

The Responsibility of Industrial Countries

Both forecasts — those of the World Bank and of the International Energy Agency — show that the energy problem, particularly

TABLE 5.8
World Oil Demand and Supply on Two Scenarios*
(mbd)

	1980	1985	1990	2000
Demand				
OECD	38.7	35-36	34-37	33-43
OPEC	2.9	4	5-6	8-9
Other LDCs	7.9	9-10	11-13	17-22
TOTAL	49.5	48-50	50-56	58-74
Supply				
OPEC	27.5	23-26	27-29	24-28
Non-OPEC	20.7	24-25	23-25	25-27
CPE Net Exports (Imp.)	1.3	1-(1)	0-(2)	0-(2)
TOTAL	49.5	48-50	50-52	49-53
Excess Demand	0	0	0-4	9-21

Source: International Energy Agency, *World Energy Outlook* (Paris, 1982).

the oil problem, which remains very acute, is very serious for the industrial countries. The OECD countries will remain highly dependent on imported oil.

The situation will become more disturbing if a revival of the world economy as we propose in this study could take place. In this assumption, the needs of energy will be greater than those projected by the two institutions. According to some other forecasts, energy needs will be twice as high as those of today. What are these countries, and particularly the highly developed countries, doing to face this situation?

It is a truism that without sufficient energy resources the acceleration of economic growth becomes impossible. Such an acceleration, furthermore, is absolutely necessary to narrow the alarming gap between the rich and the poor countries, which at present continues to widen. Let us not forget that the industrial countries now consume almost 60 percent of the world's total consumption of energy, though they account for only 22 percent of the world's population.

An increase in economic growth in the developing countries — which now consume one-tenth, and the poorest countries one-hundredth, of the energy used by the industrialized countries — is likely therefore to further complicate the energy problem.[23]

The transfer of technology to the countries of the Third World, which is generally acknowledged as being necessary, will require an ever-growing energy consumption on their part. This aspect of the energy problem is highly crucial. Any reduction in energy supplies may for this reason especially have extremely dangerous effects throughout the world. The governments of the industrial countries must take urgent measures to find new energy sources, and this not least because of their responsibilities to assist the economic development of the poor countries.

NUCLEAR FUSION: A WAY OUT?

The energy problem will find a stable solution when we are able to harness thermonuclear energy. However, it must be recognized that the harnessing of nuclear fission, which took place on December 2, 1942, and the operation of the first nuclear power plant for the production of electricity in 1950, has not produced the anticipated results.[24]

The progress made until now is not as great as had been hoped for at the beginning of the atomic era. Technical, economic, and especially ecological factors have restricted production. It is true that the production of nuclear electricity has tripled during the decade of the 1970s. But it cannot be said that this decade has been the age of nuclear electricity, as Ulf Lantzke, executive director of the International Energy Agency, has remarked. In fact, certain forecasts of installed capacities have been revised downward and some projects, including some in Western Germany and the United States have been abandoned. The Three Mile Island accident in the United States in large part shattered the confidence of public opinion in nuclear electricity and has provided arguments against its expansion.

In 1978, the perspectives for nuclear capacity growth were reduced by 50 percent in the United States, by 30 percent in Canada, by 35 percent in the Federal Republic of Germany, and by 50 percent in Japan. Only France has maintained its nuclear program unchanged, and its nuclear power plants have continued their increases. However, it is estimated that nuclear production of electricity, which at present covers 4 percent of total energy needs, might represent only 15 percent of that total in the year 2000.[25]

Nuclear Fusion: An Inexhaustible Source

The only energy source which, in our opinion, could resolve the world energy problem is nuclear fusion. This is based on a process that is today used for production of the hydrogen bomb. As we have stated in our book *Will the Atom Unite the World?*, this new energy source is destined in the long run to fundamentally change the geopolitical map of the world. When the control of nuclear fusion is achieved, an inexhaustible lower-cost energy source will be available to all countries of the world, and present-day knowledge of the atom will be only a prehistoric stage of this new era.

This gigantic source of energy will be based on the abundant supply of hydrogen contained in water. It will, as experts have said, help to "melt glaciers and irrigate deserts."

But is controlled nuclear fusion energy really part of the domain of the possible?

There are undoubtedly technical difficulties in harnessing atomic energy in this way, but the experts have for a considerable time stated that a breakthrough will not take long to achieve. At the first Geneva Conference on atomic energy, in 1975, the Indian expert Dr. Bhabha predicted that nuclear fusion could be controlled in less than 20 years. In 1970, American experts and engineers elaborated a "calendar of progress" that placed the industrial use of nuclear fusion in the 1985-95 decade.

Since that time, however, a delay in the realization of nuclear fusion for electric power production seems to have occurred. Although important progress has been made in methods of controlling fusion, what is needed in order to achieve the final objective is a closer cooperation among the large countries that are at present engaged in thermonuclear research, and the realization of the investments required to accelerate the experimental work under way.

In a recent publication[26] UNESCO has presented the opinion of two eminent specialists, Professor R. S. Pease of the United

Kingdom, president of the International Council on Fusion Research, and Dr. John Clarke, deputy director of the Fusion Energy Office in the United States, on the present state of research. These two experts are very optimistic about the possibilities of achieving the final objective. Here are their main findings:

• The results obtained in recent years are, to use their own expression, "spectacular." The problem of obtaining the very high temperatures of up to 100 million degrees Celsius required to bring about a fusion reaction — whose solution hitherto appeared utopian — has been solved in part. More than half of this temperature has been attained, that is, between 50 and 80 million degrees. According to Professor Pease, "the objective of one hundred million does not seem to present a real problem."

This prediction is reinforced by Princeton University's recent announcement (December 28, 1982) that the giant Tokamak Fusion Test Reactor will be the first in the world to generate more fusion energy than is required to produce it and is expected to produce plasma temperatures higher than 200 million degrees Fahrenheit. The Princeton experiment will demonstrate that nuclear fusion is a viable source of energy for the twenty-first century.[27] After this announcement the *Washington Post* published an article under the title "Here comes Fusion" and remarked: "Now it seems highly probable that a point will come, sometime is the next century, when this technology will be worth any price as the alternative to other and far more dangerous technologies now in prospect."[28]

• This great progress has been made in spite of a very small budgetary expenditure. The total amount spent in the world on fusion research is about $1 billion a year, mainly by the United States and the USSR. According to the two experts cited, a sum of about $10 billion would be needed in order to accelerate the U.S. program and set up an experimental power station. Has the cost of the spaceshuttle recently launched by the U.S. not been more than $10 billion?

• Controlled thermonuclear fusion has many important advantages: fewer security risks, and less serious environmental effects than "all other energy forms including solar energy." Another advantage is that fusion uses as fuel very cheap raw materials, such as hydrogen obtained from water and lithium, which exists in abundance in rocks. Another advantage, according to Professor Pease, is that "hydrogen and lithium cannot be used for military purposes."

An Inexplicable Silence

What is paradoxical is that in spite of the considerable progress made, an inexplicable silence surrounds this problem. None of the international organizations in their studies of the energy problem speak of fusion as being a realistic objective that could be attained even before the end of the century.

How can this silence be explained, especially at a moment when the energy crisis endangers the future of the world economy?

Is there a fear on the part of countries possessing abundant traditional energy sources — the United States, the USSR, and the oil-producing countries — that there would be a too rapid industrial use of thermonuclear energy?

It is evident that the first victims of the domestication of nuclear fusion would be the enterprises involved in nuclear fission. There would also be a risk of a progressive elimination of the existing traditional energy sources. It is therefore logical that the countries having conventional sources of energy are not in a hurry to accelerate their research, aiming at a rapid industrial use of nuclear fusion.

Who Will Be First
to Have a Productive Thermonuclear Bomb?

Europe and Japan, two regions that depend greatly on external energy sources, have every interest in taking the initiative in developing fusion. Euratom should, in particular, be given larger financial resources in order to participate actively in this great race.

It may be observed that the two superpowers do not show the same enthusiasm that they displayed at the beginning of the 1950s when nuclear fission was being developed. In an article I published in December 1953 in the newspaper *Le Monde*, entitled "Who Will Be the First to Have a Productive Bomb?" I wrote that no State, capitalist or communist, could delay the industrial use of atomic energy if one of the two succeeded in obtaining it. And I added that "Humanity awaits the announcement of what we might call the productive bomb, that is the liberation of this gigantic force in the service of the prosperity of the whole world." Although the editors of *Le Monde* prefaced my article with some reservations saying that this was a long-term possibility, six months later the Soviet Union announced that on June 27, 1954 they had placed in operation the first nuclear station for the production of electric power, with a capacity of 5,000 kwh.

From this moment on, other countries, especially the United States, were in the race for the construction of nuclear power stations.

In my book, *Will the Atom Unite the World?*, that examines the economic, social, and political aspects of atomic energy, I also formulated the hope that the announcement of the "productive thermonuclear bomb" would not be far off.

Let us express the ardent hope that the industrial countries participating actively in this effort will soon acquire this new technology and will be able to announce such a "productive thermonuclear bomb."

NOTES

1. The following are some recent books and studies about energy: Hans Sandsberg, *Selected studies of Energy. The next twenty years* (Cambridge, Mass.: Ballinger, 1980); T. Hoffman, & B. Johnson, *World Energy Triangle: A Strategy for Cooperation* (Cambridge, Mass.: 1980); World Bank, *Energy in the Developing Countries* (Washington, D.C., 1980); O. Noreng, *Oil Policies in the 1980's* (New York: McGraw-Hill, 1980); Economic Impact, *Oil in the World Economy*, no 3 (1980); A. Odell, and K. Rosing, *The Future of Oil-Reserves and Uses 1980-2080* (London: Kegan, 1980); M. A. Adelman, *The World Petroleum Market* (Baltimore: Johns Hopkins University Press, 1972); M. Frik, *Future Energy Consumption of the Third World* (New York: Pergamon, 1982); W. L. Kohl, *After the Second Oil Crisis* (Lexington, Mass.: Heath, 1982); R. Mabro, *World Energy. Issues and Policies* (New York: Oxford University Press, 1982); International Energy Agency, Various publications and particularly *Energy Outlook* (Paris: OECD, 1982).

2. The way in which the demand for energy reacts to price increases has been examined in the OECD study, "The Demand for Energy," Working Party No 4, March 27, 1980 and in various publications by the International Energy Agency.

3. OECD, International Energy Agency, *World Energy Outlook*, Summary, (Paris, 1982), p. 9.

4. Angelos Angelopoulos, *For a New Policy of International Development* (New York: Praeger, 1977), p. 1 *et seq*.

5. OECD, *For Full Employment and Price Stability* (McCracken Report), June 1979, pp. 75-76.

6. On the evolution of the oil crisis, see the study by Alain Murcier entitled "Pétrole, la révolution de 20 ans," in *l'Expansion*, November 7, 1980, p. 133 *et seq*.

7. IMF, *Bulletin*, February 25, 1980, p. 53.

8. Between the beginning of 1974 and the end of 1978 the dollar was devalued in relation to other currencies, see chapter 1.

9. World Bank, *World Development Report* (Washington, 1980), p. 17.

10. Taxes on gasoline alone — without counting other taxes on petroleum products — represented in 1977 some 8.37 percent of the total fiscal receipts of the state in Italy, 4.18 percent in France and 3.66 percent in the Fed. Rep. of Germany (IMF, *Bulletin*, January 25, 1980, p. 54).

11. IMF, *World Economic Outlook*, 1980, p. 95.

12. The Brandt Commission commented as follows on the role of oil: "It is not oil prices which are responsible for all these troubles, but apparently the management of oil has become a grave problem for the world economy" (Brandt Commission, *Report*, p. 72).

13. IMF, *World Economic Outlook*, 1982, p. 160.

14. IMF, *World Economic Outlook*, p. 165.

15. These countries are:

Algeria	Kuwait	Qatar
Indonesia	Libya	Saudi Arabia
Iran	Nigeria	United Arab Emirates
Iraq	Oman	Venezuela

16. *Business Week*, November 19, 1979.

17. OECD, *World Energy Outlook*, (Paris, 1982), p. 9.

18. Ibid., p. 37.

19. North Sea Oil is now reaching a production level of 2 million barrels a day, but its cost of extraction is higher than that of Middle East Oil.

20. Regarding Mexico, proved reserves are already estimated at 50 billion barrels, which would make this country the sixth largest producer in the world. At present, production is 29 million barrels per day, of which 1 million is exported, bringing a return of almost $11 billion in 1980.

21. A breakdown, provided by the Shell Oil Company, of the price of a barrel of refined oil sold in Europe between 1973 and 1978 in U.S. dollars follows:

	1973	1978
Revenue of the producing countries	2.60	13.00
Cost of production	0.251	0.50
Transport to Rotterdam	0.85	1.00
Requiring and distribution	2.75	5.35
Revenue of the importing country	0.60	13.55
Oil sellers' margin	0.60	0.55
Total	7.651	33.80

22. OECD (Paris), 1982.

23. On the energy problem as it concerns particularly the progress of the developing countries up to the year 2000, see the article by Wolfgang Sassi, *Scientific American*, September 1980, pp. 107 *et seq*.

24. Regarding the evolution of nuclear energy and its economic and social aspects, see my book *L'Atome unira-t-il le monde?*, published by Pichon and Durand Auzias (Paris, 1955) and the English edition entitled *Will the Atom Unite the World?* published by Bodlay Head (London, 1957).

25. Data from "Nuclear Energy in the year 2000," in the OECD *Observer*, November 1980, p. 42.

26. UNESCO, *Informations*, no 747 (1979).

27. See *International Herald Tribune*, December 30, 1982.

28. Ibid., January 8, 1983.

6

**WHY A NEW GLOBAL
ECONOMIC POLICY
IS NEEDED**

THE INTERDEPENDENCE OF ECONOMIES IN THE WORLD
REQUIRES A GLOBAL MANAGEMENT STRATEGY

The presentation we made in the preceding chapters provides a disappointing balance sheet of the world economy's condition in the period 1974-82. If present policy continues without radical changes, then prospects for the decades to come appear, as has been already shown, very gloomy indeed. The further pursuit of present policies will lead to economic chaos.

The present condition of the world economy requires a growth and development strategy and one that would include the countries of the whole world. This is all the more necessary as there is a close and increasing interdependence in economic activity and international financing among the countries of the globe. A consequence of this interdependence is that the problems of one country become world problems and their solution can only be sought within this wide international framework.

The significance of this factor of interdependence has been repeatedly underlined in summit meetings of the world's leading statesmen, in resolutions of the United Nations, and in studies of international organizations.[1] The Willy Brandt Commission, also, has shown in its report how the problems of Northern countries are closely linked with those of the South and how a constructive international cooperation serves the interests of all countries of the world.

Characteristic of this close interdependence among industrial and developing countries is the sharp drop in the GNP growth of the industrial countries from 0.5 percent in 1982 to only an estimated 1.5 percent in 1983. This reduction is explained, according to the OECD last *Economic Outlook* (December 1982), by the unexpectedly sharp drop in demand for OECD imports in developing and OPEC countries and by the depressed level of activity in Europe.

The success of new policies will depend on the existence of a sincere, coherent, and dynamic collaboration among all countries — the industrial, the developing, and the oil-exporting.

Only a new global strategy, based on a worldwide plan for the development of world resources, using present-day technology, can meet the double challenge of our time; combating misery and poverty and lifting the world economy out of its present impasse.

The Basic Principles

In order to develop a new international growth and employment strategy, it is necessary to start with certain basic principles, the most important of which are:

• The recognition that prosperity must be universal and that the rich countries will not be able to survive in the long run as islands in the middle of an ocean of misery. As the United Nations General Assembly has stated, "economic and social progress is a common responsibility, which should be shared by the international community as a whole."

• A larger, more equitable, and more human content should be given to economic development. The development objective requires not only the accumulation of goods but also, and primarily, the promotion of the interests of the human being as an integral whole. Development is thus a process of structural change in the economic, social, political, and cultural domains. Furthermore, development must be carried out for the benefit of all and not of a small minority. It is a collective effort and its fruits must be equitably distributed among all.

A new growth and development strategy requires a new way of thinking and must be based on the "New World Economic Order" and the "Charter of the Rights and Duties of States" that were adopted by the United Nations General Assembly in 1974.[2]

According to Resolution 3201 (S.VI), adopted by the General Assembly at its sixth special session in May 1974, the existing economic order, which "was characterized by inequality, domination, dependence, narrow self-interest and segmentation," must be replaced "by a new order based on equity, sovereign equality, interdependence, common interest and cooperation among states irrespective of their economic and social systems. . . . The new order would extend international cooperation and would be geared fully toward utilizing the world's potential for rapid social and economic advance."

The Negative Attitudes of Industrialized Countries

Unfortunately, the adoption of United Nations resolutions concerning the "New World Economic Order" and the "Chapter of Rights and Duties of States" was not favorably received by some industrial countries.[3] The policy followed since then has shown that the spirit of these resolutions has not yet met with universal approval. Seven years after the adoption of the resolution for a new international economic order, "progress has been negligible," according to a recent study of the United Nations.[4]

Successive summit meetings of statesmen, representing the developed and developing countries, held between 1975 and 1982 on the international economic situation have shown a lack of agreement on application of the principle of international solidarity. Nevertheless, several factors of great significance favor the adoption of a new development strategy. The most important of these (to be discussed briefly in the following paragraphs) are:

1. Interdependence with respect to raw materials.
2. The need for investments on an international scale, especially investments in energy.
3. The political strength of the Third World on the international scene.
4. Recognition of the unfavorable consequences of the absence of international cooperation.
5. The advent of the atomic era, which requires joint efforts on a worldwide scale for a constructive cooperation.

INTERDEPENDENCE AND THE PROBLEM
OF RAW MATERIALS

The prosperity of the industrial countries depends on the progress of the developing countries. This dependence assumes a double form. On the one hand, the industrial countries import a great quantity of products from the developing countries. On the other hand, some 23 percent of the production of the countries of the European Community, for example, goes to non-oil-producing developing countries. Between 1963 and 1979, industrial countries registered a great surplus in their trade accounts with non-oil-producing developing countries that rose from $25 billion to $60 billion during this period.[5] Thus the economic activity of the industrial countries depends to a great extent on the developing countries, particularly with respect to raw materials. This has been emphasized in a recent study by the Commission of the European Communities.[6]

According to this study, the known reserves of raw materials are located as follows:

• 44 percent of the world total are situated in the industrial countries, and 94 percent of these are in the United States, Canada, Australia, and South Africa;

• 20 percent are in the Eastern countries, of which 82 percent are in the Soviet Union;

• 33 percent are situated in the Third World, of which 69 percent are in six countries (Brazil, 25 percent; Chile, 19 percent; Indonesia, 7 percent; Zaire, Guinea, and India, 6 percent each).

Raw Material Requirements:
Europe and the United States

According to estimates by the European Commission, the Community must import 75 percent of the raw materials it needs, and Japan 90 percent. With respect to certain raw materials, the dependence of the Community is even greater. It is 99 percent for manganese and platinum, which come especially from South Africa and the USSR, and the same for chrome, which is found almost entirely in South Africa and Zimbabwe. Estimates made by the services of the Federal Republic of Germany indicate that a lack of chrome would render one and a half million workers unemployed within three months.

The external dependence of the United States is on the whole less than that of other Western countries. Only 25 percent of its raw material needs come from other countries. Nevertheless, the dependence of the United States on foreign supplies of certain raw materials of strategic importance is very large.[7]

The dependence of the large industrial countries for externally supplied raw materials leads them to maintain strategic stockpiles[8] and to follow a common policy in order to ensure supplies so necessary to the functioning of their economies. This interdependence shows how greatly needed is a cooperation between the industrial countries and the countries of the Third World. It also shows that the absence of a rational and suitable organization of international exchanges may create an explosive situation full of risks and rivalries. The precedent of the two oil crises should indicate that a close international cooperation is a prerequisite to prosperity and peace, especially now when developing countries begin to be aware of and to exercise their economic and political power.[9]

Raw Material Prices: A Continuing Issue

Fluctuations in prices of raw materials hamper the functioning of the world economy, and undermine economic and social progress of all the countries in the world. Thus, a price agreement has long been a vital need for the developing countries. According to estimates by the Commission of the European Communities, trade in raw materials represents only 4 percent of the GDP in the importing Community countries, but accounts for up to 75 percent of the income of certain of the exporting developing countries. An average increase of 50 percent in the prices of raw materials would bring to the Third World countries, according to the Commission, supplementary resources "three times higher than the amount at present devoted to development assistance." The European Community has stated its belief that an increase in the prices of raw materials could be beneficial for the world economy as a whole. It is more than certain that the proceeds from such a price increase would, in turn, result in increasing the imports of these countries and would thereby have favorable repercussions on the economic activity of the exporting industrial countries. This, in fact, has been the case with oil, where following the increase in prices, an appreciable increase in imports from the industrialized countries took place.

Contrary to original expectations, the growth in trade between old and new industrial countries (Brazil, Mexico, Korea, Hong Kong, Taiwan, Singapore, Spain, Greece, Portugal, Yugoslavia) resulted according to OECD estimates, in the creation, between 1963 and 1977 alone, of more than one half million new jobs.[10]

THE NEED FOR LARGE INVESTMENTS ON A WORLDWIDE SCALE, PARTICULARLY IN THE ENERGY SECTOR

All countries must undertake large investments in the vital sectors of their economies. This must be done with foresight and in full cognizance of the consequences of such actions for poor as well as for rich countries. To this end, an international organization should be given the task of overseeing these investments. This is necessary both in order to accelerate world economic and social progress and to help ensure an equitable distribution of investments among countries.

Investments in Minerals

We will limit ourselves here to a brief indication of the significance of two forms of investments: in mineral raw materials, for which the West is 75 percent dependent on foreign supplies, as we have seen, and in energy, which is a major determinant of economic growth and development in general.

It is clear that industrial countries must secure a sufficient volume of investment in mining development where a significant shortage of investment has been observed during the last few years. As a study of the European Community notes, a substantial increase in mineral prices during the 1980s may be expected to occur because of the low level of investment in mining today.[11]

One example: for the six main metals − iron, copper, zinc, aluminum, nickel and lead − the annual investments needed to ensure only a modest increase in consumption were estimated by the United Nations at $12 billion (1975 value). This amount is much higher than the investments made in recent years. It is estimated that the investments in mineral production made by European companies alone were very small between 1966 and 1977, not exceeding $600 million a year; furthermore, these investments were geographically maldistributed.

The weakness of investments in mineral production and consequently the reduction in output will continue to bring about upward pressures on prices. In the absence of international agreements, these rises may become irregular and uncontrollable and have harmful effects on the world economy, even though in the short run they may benefit the producers.

Investments in Energy

Another problem of great importance for economic growth is the need for new sources of energy. The acceleration of this search requires massive investments especially in order to increase coal and natural gas extraction and to develop new energy sources.[12] Among these sources is solar energy, which is in an advanced stage of experimentation, as are geothermic energy and other sources. Furthermore, a high priority must be given to the acceleration of research in the nuclear field, especially to the application of thermo-nuclear energy, that is, fusion, a subject that has been examined in Chapter 5. The acceleration of this research requires important investments on international scale.

Investments in Infrastructure

The large and indispensable investments required not only in the fields already mentioned but also in the infrastructures of the developing countries (roads, railways, dams, electric power stations, health, education, etc.) cannot be realized except through the application of policies on an international scale.

Moreover, the elementary requirements of the populations of the poor countries are so great and the need for their satisfaction is so urgent, that no delay can be afforded in making the necessary investments to this end.[13] It is a paradox of our times that developing countries, and particularly countries like China, India, and regions of Africa, have immense unsatisfied needs for capital and other goods, while in the industrial countries an excess supply of the same goods remains.

THE POLITICAL STRENGTH OF THE THIRD WORLD

Another factor that makes the adoption of a worldwide development strategy necessary is that the Third World is already playing a very important role on the international political scene. Any attempt to delay the adoption of such a strategy will have dangerous consequences for political stability in the world as well as for economic welfare.

The economic development of the Third World is based on the very strong determination of their people. The governments of these countries wish essentially to overcome the gap that separates them from the industrial countries and to accomplish this task at a rate faster than ever before.

It is a characteristic of our times that during the periods 1968-72 and 1973-80, while the GNP of industrial countries dropped from an annual growth rate of 4.5 to 3.1 percent, the growth rate of the GNP of the non-oil developing countries remained rather constant (from 5.8 to 5.2 percent). This, perhaps, represents a refutation of the view that the rate of growth of the developing countries is inexorably linked to the rate of growth of the industrial countries.[14]

Indeed this view is dangerous. The industrial countries cannot prevent the economic growth of the Third World. A hostile or negative attitude on the part of the industrial countries is likely to have consequences harmful to their own interests, to create an unhealthy reaction that can lead to civil conflicts, and even to become one of the possible causes of wars between poor and rich countries.

We recall again what the great scientist Robert Oppenheimer said shortly before he died: "When immense populations which today live on the border of famine and misery become aware of their situation and of ours, then I fear what may happen."

Factors Favoring Development

Three factors favor a rapid development of the Third World:[15]

1. The enormous human and material potential of these countries;

2. The important dynamic role, at all levels, of young people and the need for measures in their economic favor;

3. The immense scientific and technological progress recently realized, which will continue to grow over time.

While these factors favor the development of the Third World, the actual prospects will depend on the extent to which international cooperation, and the appropriate level of financing will be forthcoming.

As we know, the global population, which now stands at 4.6 billion is increasing by 77 million per year and will reach, according to the projections of the United Nations, 6.1 billion by the year 2000. The changes in the distribution of population between 1975 and 2000 are shown in Figure 6.1. The increase is faster in the developing than in the industrial countries. The table below shows the expected increase between 1980 and 2000 for certain regions.

The most rapid increase in the population between 1980 and 2000 is expected to take place in Africa with 70 percent followed by Latin America with 45 percent. Furthermore, the young population will increase in the developing countries by 34 percent between these two periods, that is from 665 to 893 million, while in the industrial countries the young population will diminish by 8 percent, from 192 million in 1980 to 176 million in the year 2000.[16]

Moreover, by the year 2000, the number of workers will be on the order of 3.5 billion in the Third World countries, whereas in the Western countries it will be only 600 million. In other words, 83 persons out of every 100 of working age will be living in the regions that are now underdeveloped. Can the gravity of this situation be safely ignored? One thing is certain — there will be economic and social progress in the Third World that will tend to give it a more powerful economic and social position during the next century. Indeed, as we have stated in the Introduction, while the nineteenth century can be said to have been the age of Europe, and the twentieth

Geographic Regions	Population (in millions)		Percent increase
	1980	2000	
North America	256	286	12
Europe	488	511	5
UR-SS	270	302	12
Latin America	378	549	45
Asia	1,671	2,328	39
China	1,000	1,200	20
Africa	498	847	70

Source: U.S. News and World Report, August 22, 1982.

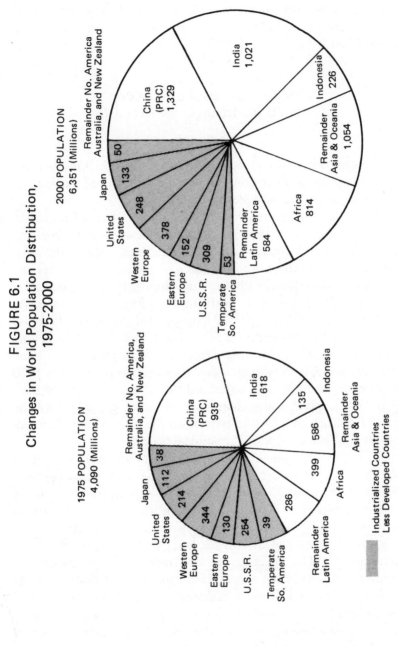

FIGURE 6.1
Changes in World Population Distribution,
1975-2000

2000 POPULATION
6,351 (Millions)

1975 POPULATION
4,090 (Millions)

Industrialized Countries
Less Developed Countries

Source: The Global 2000 Report to the President, The Technical Report, Volume Two.

119

century that of the United States and the Soviet Union, the twenty-first century is likely to be the age of the Third World of Asia, Africa, and South/Latin America.

ABSENCE OF COOPERATION
LEADS TO RUINOUS COMPETITION

The continuation of the policies now in force will result inevitably in an intense competition among all countries and particularly among the industrial countries of the West.

As has already been pointed out, the number of countries participating in world production and trade is steadily increasing and competition in world markets is intensifying. In addition to the older industrial countries, there are now the new industrial countries and other Third World countries that are developing their industries and their exports. The network of world trade in its present complexity is depicted in Figure 6.2 provided by the International Monetary Fund. However, the competition from Third World countries is only beginning; it will accelerate over time and the importance of these countries in world trade will increase. While between 1950 and 1970 the developing countries accounted only for 7 to 8 percent of total world industrial production, their share is expected to rise by the end of the century to 17 or 18 percent of the total, thereby exceeding even that of the European Economic Community.

Such a redistribution of industrial production could constitute a danger for the old industrial countries, if the world economy were to remain stagnant, and could also lead to a protectionist war. In fact, whereas before 1974 we witnessed an uninterrupted reduction in customs barriers, since that year we have been observing in developed countries a reversal of this tendency and a continuous rise in protectionism.[17] The meeting of 88 trade ministers in Geneva (November 1982) has been a near-fiasco and showed that free trade is in terrible trouble. Economic recession and trade protection feed on one another.

If the world economy remains stagnant, the struggle to conquer new markets will be a sharp, cutthroat competition, without principles or limitations. In such a world, the expansion of one country's

FIGURE 6.2
World Trade Flows, 1981
(billion U.S. dollars)

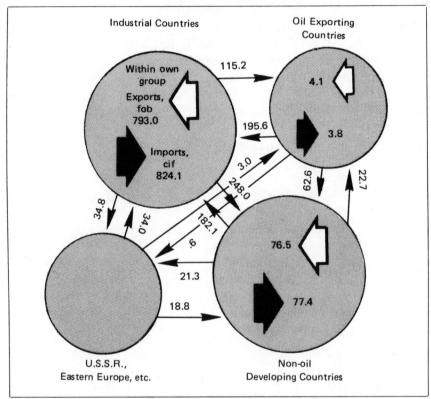

Source: IMF Survey, May 1982.

exports will inevitably mean the decline of a competitor's sales, leading to a confrontation among nations.

The United States, Europe and Japan

Strong competition among the United States, the European Community, and Japan — leaving aside the USSR and the Eastern countries — is already visible. This competition will become more acute as time passes.

Where can this competition among the major industrial countries lead us? At present, Japan is clearly leading.[19] Favored by many factors — qualified but much cheaper labor, a very structured organization of production, continuously increasing investments in automation and the large-scale production of robots, and by small military expenditures — Japan is likely to become the major world power at the sunset of the twentieth century.

According to American estimates, the economic growth of Japan in the decade of the 1980s will be two times greater than that of the other industrial countries, as shown in the following table:[20]

GNP in million dollars (1980)

Country	1980	1990	Average Growth Rate (%)	Increase (%)
United States	2,629	3,568	3.1	+35.7
Common Market	2,463	3,278	2.9	+33.1
USSR	1,401	1,938	3.3	+38.3
Japan	1,053	1,765	5.3	+67.6

Thus Japan is expected to progress more rapidly than the other highly industrial countries, and if this progress continues, by the year 2025, Japan would have a higher national income than the United States.

This forecast may, in fact, be surpassed, considering that the actual growth rates in the United States and the Common Market are below those indicated. For the decade 1980-90 the growth of the U.S. and the Common Market economies may not exceed 2 percent if present economic policies continue; on the other hand, for reasons already stated, Japan's growth rate may reach and even surpass the forecast rate of 5.3 percent. Presently, unemployment and inflation in Japan are 2.1 and 3.6 percent respectively, while in the European Community the corresponding figures are 10 and 12 percent.

In order to absorb the "surplus" of its production, Japan has given absolute priority to an increase in its exports. In 1980 exports to the European Community increased by 25 percent while in the same year, the Community's exports to Japan increased by only 2.8 percent. And this is not all. There is a strong Japanese wish to put down roots in the Western and Asian countries by making direct investments there as well. Globally, the cumulative total of Japanese investments in overseas countries since the decade of the 1950s reached the amount of $33 billion, according to a report by the Japanese Organization for Foreign Trade (JETRO).

This large sum is expected to increase fourfold by 1990 according to The Economic Research Center of Tokyo, and by then to have reached 155 billion dollars.[21] In order to appreciate the importance of such investments we may note that the total foreign investments of the United States in 1980 were $193 billion. Thus the penetration by Japan of the international direct investment scene is taking place to the disadvantage of the other industrial countries and in particular, of the United States and Europe.

THE ATOMIC ERA IMPOSES A CONSTRUCTIVE COOPERATION

Besides all the aforementioned reasons justifying the need for a new development strategy, there is another major reason requiring a revision of the international policy of all countries and particularly that of the superpowers. That is the advent of the atomic age, which, with all its positive and negative repercussions, constitutes a new major factor in human calculations and requires new orientations leading to a constructive cooperation among all peoples of the world.

As we have shown in a previous book[22] and as we have underlined in Chapter 5, the appearance of nuclear and thermonuclear energy is destined, in the long run, to bring about profound changes in the structure of the economy and of society on an international scale. It is even destined to bring about changes in the geopolitical map of the world.

If, as we said, thermonuclear energy were to be harnessed about the end of the century, the repercussions on the development of Third World countries would be of major importance for the utilization of their economic potential. Thus, thanks to this new energy, those regions that produce raw materials but cannot actually exploit them, will henceforth be able to manufacture final products on the spot and export them.

If we accept that war in the atomic age is an "inconceivable eventuality," the "peaceful coexistence" between the two super-powers is a necessity. Winston Churchill, speaking on June 8, 1954 at a gathering of English-speaking peoples, declared that duty as well as interest dictate that the communists and the free world must make an effort to live together peacefully.

However, this coexistence must be active and constructive and not "static." This latter attitude leads to cold war, to economic crises, and to local conflicts, with all the risks involved for world peace.

Mistrust Toward Coexistence

There are many, however, who view the policy of peaceful coexistence with mistrust. They regard it as nothing more than a "Trojan horse" or a "prolonged respite" from which the Soviet Union alone stands to benefit. They maintain that the communist leaders, notwithstanding their peace propaganda and "campaigns of smiles," are not for one moment losing sight of their ultimate goal, which is the triumph of revolution throughout the world. They believe, further, that the communists will take every possible tactical and strategic advantage of the period of peaceful coexistence in order to attain that goal, which is the ultimate victory of communism. They point out the significance of such events as the Soviet intervention in Hungary in October 1956, in Czechoslovakia, and more recently in Afghanistan.

This point of view is not, indeed, entirely without foundation. Marxist-Leninist philosophy postulates the inevitable victory of communism through the collapse of capitalism.

However, the driving force for the expansion of communism is found less in ideology and more in the social conditions of every country. The chances of communist infiltration are greatest in those countries where, through the apathy or ineptitude of governments, the economic and social situation deteriorates instead of improving; where social injustice increases instead of diminishing; where people who aspire to independence are condemned to continue to live under foreign domination. Wherever these conditions exist, revolutionary movements develop, civil wars break out, and an atmosphere favorable to the propagation of communism is created.

It is certain that misery, poverty, and inequality remain the basic causes of political troubles and social conflicts in underdeveloped regions. Only a raising of the standard of living of the populations of these regions may prevent these troubles and the expansion of communism. Tibor Mende, a specialist on Asiatic countries, who has studied the problems of these countries on the spot, has this to say: "The only defence [against communism] can be assured by means of reforms, economic aid, supplies of foodstuffs, better organization and a more equitable distribution of the national income."[23]

If only a small part of the GNP of industrial countries were to be granted to developing countries, as we propose in Chapter 8 of this study, and were to be utilized to improve their very low standard of living, the economic and political situation would be entirely different. If freedom of expression and a respect for the human personality, which constitute the effective weapons of Western countries, were accompanied by social reform, by greater economic, social and cultural progress, then the chances for the expansion of communism would be very limited indeed. Only the adoption of a new development strategy, aiming at the establishment of a new world economic order, can fight hunger and poverty and ensure prosperity as well as peace in the world.

This then is the form of coexistence that is offered to us today. We must accept it or reject it. If we accept it, we must do so with our eyes open to all its implications: there must be no "coexistence in fear" or "coexistence in misunderstanding," but, in the words of Pope Pius XII, a "coexistence in truth." If, after examining the arguments for and against it we come to the conclusion that a policy of coexistence is not merely a necessity but the only possible way of dispelling the menace that hangs over the future, this policy must be our aim. We must adopt a new way of thinking out the problems of our time; their solution must be sought through constructive cooperation on an international scale.

All these factors require a new economic global management strategy for a balanced development between all countries of the world. Without such a strategy, a chain of successive recessions, whose consequences may seriously shake the foundations of the present economic and financial structure, will ensue.

NOTES

1. We note some studies about interdependence: Richard Cooper, *The Economics of Interdependence* (New York: McGraw-Hill, 1968; Fred Bergsten, *Managing International Economic Interdependence* (Lexington Boot Books, 1977); V. Mahler, *Dependency Approaches to International Political Economy* (New York: Columbia University Press, 1980); OECD, *From Marshall Plan to Global Interdependence* (Paris, 1978); UNESCO, *Perceptions de l'Interdependance mondiale* (Paris, 1978); Fr. Perroux, *Interdépendance des Nations* (Paris: Aubier, 1969); F. Rosenau, *The Study of Global Interdependence* (New York: Nicholas, 1982); Robert McNamarra, *Economic Interdependence and Global Poverty*, the first Barbara Ward Memorial Lecture, Baltimore, 1982.

2. Resolutions on a "New World Economic Order" and a "Charter of the Rights and Duties of States" were adopted by a substantial majority of countries at the twenty-ninth General Assembly of the United Nations, held from September 17 to December 18, 1974. See also, United Nations, *Towards the New International Economic Order* (New York, 1982).

3. The resolutions were adopted in December 1974 by 120 members of the United Nations, despite the opposition or reservations of developed countries, 6 of which voted against and 10 abstained.

4. United Nations, *Towards a New International Economic Order* (New York, 1982), p. 68.

5. OECD, *Observer*, January 1982, p. 9.

6. *The Challenge of Raw Materials* (Le Défi des Matières Premières), January 1981. An interesting analysis of the problem of raw materials may also be found in a series of articles by specialists, published in two issues of *Le Monde Diplomatique* (Paris), in February and March, 1981 under the title "The Race for Mineral Resources." This analysis refers to all aspects of the problem of raw materials. On the same subject, see a study in OECD, *Observer*, no. 100 (September 1979), and the publication of the Commission of the European Communities, *Europe and the Third World; A Study of Interdependence* (Brussels, 1979).

7. The magazine *Business Week* of April 6, 1981 has published a table, reproduced here, based on information from the U.S. Bureau of Mines. It shows a critical situation with respect to dependence on foreign sources for certain critical minerals.

America's foreign sources for 10 critical minerals
(percentage)

Bauxite	Aluminum	94	Jamaica, Guinea, Surinam
Chromium	Ferroalloys	91	South Africa, Soviet Union
Cobalt	Superalloys, mainly for turbine engines	93	Zaire, Belgium, Luxembourg, Zambia
Columbium	Ferroalloys	100	Brazil
Manganese	Steel	97	Gabon, South Africa
Nickel	Steel	73	Canada
Platinum group	Catalysts	87	South Africa, Soviet Union
Rutile	Pigments, metals	100	Australia
Tantalum	Electronic components	97	Thailand
Titanium	Mainly aerospace components	47	Japan, Soviet Union

Data: U.S. Bureau of Mines

Source: *Business Week*, April 6, 1981.

8. According to the Federal Agency for Geopolitical Studies in the United States, reserves of natural gas, which were 16.820 billion cubic meters, represented 30 years' supply at present consumption rates. Oil reserves are estimated at 83 billion barrels or 13 years of present consumption (see *Le Monde*, March 17, 1981).

9. A characteristic example of this attitude is the declaration of a representative of the Hong Kong government, who stated with respect to the policies of the industrial countries on textiles that: "The developing countries have not forgotten the disastrous effects of this policy (imposing limits on textile imports), and they will enter the forthcoming negotiations with a cohesion which they have not hitherto shown" (see *Le Figaro*, April 17, 1981).

10. See OECD, *Observer*, no. 99 (July 1979).

11. EEC, *The Challenge of Raw Materials* (Brussels, 1981).

12. This point was underlined during the Versailles Summit meeting in June 1982 by France's President François Mitterand, in a report submitted on Technology, Employment and Development.

13. World Bank, *Meeting Basic Needs: An Overview*, September 1980.

14. Reference is made to a recent study by Morris Goldstein and M. Khan, "Effects of the Slowdown in Industrial Countries on Growth in Non-Oil Developing Countries," International Monetary Fund, 1982.

15. This subject has been developed in my book, *Le Tiers Monde Face aux Pays Riches*, p. 165 *et seq*.

16. International Labour Organization, 68th session, Geneva, 1982, p. 6.

17. On this subject, see S. Page, "The Revival of Protectionism and its Consequences for Europe," in *The Journal of Common Market Studies* (Oxford), September 1981.

18. A very interesting analysis of the problems of free trade and protectionism is given by the *Economist* (London) December 25, 1982.

19. In an interview granted to the French Magazine *Le Point* (December 29, 1980) an experienced Japanese industrialist, M. Konosuke Matsushita, made the following statement: "In a certain way and at a certain moment, Japan will take the leadership of the great world family. This will be thanks to electronics . . . because in this domain Japan will be in the forefront of world knowledge."

20. See *U.S. News and World Report*, February 9, 1981.

21. In 1981 alone, Japan's direct investments abroad reached the record level of $8.9 billion according to the Japanese Ministry of Finance. This represents an increase of 90 percent over the preceding year (see *Le Monde*, June 9, 1982). See also, M. Sakkamoto, "Le Japon vers le XXe siècle," in *Futurites 2000*, (May 1979).

22. A. Angelopoulos, *Will the Atom Unite the World? Economic, Social and Political Aspects of the Atomic Age* (London: Bodlay Head, 1957). This book was published after the first atomic conference in Geneva, in 1955.

23. Tibor Mende, "Le Sud-Est asiatique entre deux mondes" (Paris, 1954).

7

FOR KEYNESIANISM ON
A WORLD SCALE

THE SUCCESS OF KEYNESIAN POLICY
FOR A QUARTER CENTURY

The reasons we have put forward in the preceding chapters have shown the necessity of a new development strategy whose objective should be the establishment of a new world economic order.

The next question is how to follow a new policy calculated to bring about the realization of this objective.

What should such a policy be like? Is the Keynesian system, that has yielded so many positive results for a quarter century, no longer valid? And if that is the case, what are the factors that have undermined its validity? Furthermore, will a readjustment of the principles of the Keynesian theory on an international scale give it a new validity?[1]

These are the questions we will try to examine in the present chapter.

Between 1945 and 1972 the Western countries were able to apply a policy that allowed them over this long period to attain and maintain sustained economic growth of their GNPs (5 percent on average) and also a real improvement in living conditions for their people. How was it possible for these countries not only to ensure full employment during this time but also — in the countries of industrialized Western Europe — to find places for 2 million immigrant workers? Why for this long period was the Keynesian theory so effective in contributing to economic and social progress?

The Genesis of the Keynesian Revolution

When the John Maynard Keynes's book *The General Theory of Employment, Interest and Money* appeared in 1936, the effects of the great world economic crisis of 1928 still remained very deeply marked in the economic system. In most of the Industrial countries, unemployment continued at a high rate. The United Kingdom, where unemployment had been endemic since 1922, still had in 1937 more than 1.5 million workers without jobs.

Conscious of the catastrophic effects of this crisis, Keynes violently criticized governments for the policies they were applying. In publishing his book he wished to present a realistic interpretation of the functioning of the economy and to propose a new policy aimed at achieving a better world. As soon as the book appeared, it caused a veritable revolution in the science of economics: a revolution in principles, methods, and in policies.

Keynes was not only a theoretical economist or a simple university professor; he was also a man endowed with a rich culture. He was a pragmatist, well acquainted with the political and economic realities of his time. He sought to understand and explain economic phenomena as a whole against the background of the evolution of the era in which he lived. Before becoming a governor of the Bank of England, he had been an economic adviser to the government. In opposition to the fundamental dogmas of the classical school of economists, he developed a new general theory, which, after the Second World War, became the foundation of the economic policy of the Western countries. "The Keynesian revolution," wrote J. K. Galbraith in 1965 in his preface to the American edition, "was from a social viewpoint one of the greatest accomplishments of our times."

Keynes did not underestimate the reactions of the "establishment" of the time to his theories. Certain of his critics characterized them, when his book was published, as "surprising" and "unortho-dox." Keynes found these reactions natural. As he wrote in the preface to his book, "the difficulty is not in understanding new ideas but to escape from old ideas which have their roots in all corners of the minds of people who have been formed in the same way as most of us!" The remark of Keynes is valid whenever a divorce between theory and reality exists, as in certain cases of social conflict.

Keynes foresaw the influence of his theory even before the publication of his book. In a letter that he sent to his friend George Bernard Shaw on New Year's Day, 1935, he wrote in a character-istic way: "I believe myself to be writing a book on economic theory which will largely revolutionize − not I suppose at once but in the course of the next ten years − the way the world thinks about economic problems. . . . I know that you will not believe me at the present time. As far as I am concerned, this is not a hope which I express but a certainty."[2]

Keynes was right. His book was truly revolutionary. "It had the effect of a bomb," to use the expression of R. Halbroner.[3] It has had an influence on economic science comparable to other revolu-tionary writings such as the *Wealth of Nations* of Adam Smith and *Capital* of Karl Marx.

Some Principles of the Keynesian Theory

In order to appreciate the contribution of the Keynesian theory, the economic situation prevailing in the 1930s and the classical theories in force at that time to combat economic depression must be remembered. These classical theories, based on the marginal utility theory precepts, had concluded that all unemployment was voluntary. This was so, the theories explained, because each supplier of labor offered as many labor-hours of work of his time as it took to equalize the marginal disutility of work to the marginal utility of the wage rate. Thus the remedies recommended were limited to use of the automatic market regulatory mechanism without any inter-vention by the State.

How is it possible then, that theories developed in the midst of a period that was characterized by one of the severest situations of unemployment and misery in contemporary history could have all, with monotonous uniformity, reached the conclusion that all unemployment is self-generated by the workers withholding further labor and that, therefore, it is purely voluntary? It is this very paradox, perhaps, that made Keynes once write that a lot of policy-makers see two parallel lines cross and they scold them for crossing instead of perceiving that the lines might not be parallel in the first place.

Keynes, rejecting the classical theories whose application had led to a complete failure of the existing economic system, argued that the cause of unemployment was not the attitudes of the workers in asking for higher wages, but rather those of the capital-holders who did not spend enough and who hoarded their savings instead of investing them. He recommended the intervention of the State, which through budgetary, tax, social, and monetary means could and should revive economic activity.

A Macroeconomic Vision of the Economy as a Whole

The main elements of the Keynesian theory that particularly concern the problem of employment and production are based on a macroeconomic understanding of the economy and of its working mechanism as an interlocking entity rather than as a partitioned, semiindependent set of groups as was basically assumed under the pre-Keynesian doctrines.

It was for this reason that Keynes used the term "General Theory" in the title of his book. In the preface to the French edition, published in January 1939, three years after the first English edition, he himself wrote: "We have given to our theory the name 'General Theory' because by that term we have wished to indicate that we have mainly in view the functioning of the economic system as a whole, that we envisage global income, global profits, global production, global employment, global investment, and global savings rather than the incomes of enterprises and of individuals considered in isolation."

This broad vision of Keynes with respect to the economy as a whole is one of the main characteristics of his theory, and it consequently forms the framework for a coordinated linkage of various economic factors. Such coordination is necessary because a close interdependence exists between production, employment and income. The level of employment is determined by the level of production, which in turn depends on an "effective demand" that is composed of consumption demand and investment demand.

Consumption demand
+ → effective → Production → Employment →
investment demand   demand   level   level

income → demand → ...
payments

According to Keynes, the existence of an adequate "effective demand" and the "quality between savings and investment" constitute the primordial condition for a rational operation of the economic system and the maintenance of an economic balance that will ensure full employment. If "effective demand," which is made up of consumption and investment demand, is insufficient, the factors of production will not be fully utilized and consequently the level of employment will be lowered and workers will be without jobs.

Now, if a part of the population holds back its expenditures on consumption, it is necessary, in order to safeguard the economic balance, that other parts of the population acquire an additional purchasing power, thereby offsetting the lack of expenditure and absorbing excess production. If this does not happen, the fall in demand will lead to a drop in production and consequently to underemployment and unemployment. To avoid this, the State must intervene — according to Keynes — raising the "propensity to consume" of the economically poorest classes by an appropriate social policy. This policy should aim at a redistribution of income within the country in order to improve living conditions for the people, thus creating new consumers to absorb the goods produced. As Joan Robinson, a disciple of Keynes who has described the Keynesian theory very clearly has stated, income, while being a source of expenditures, is also the product of expenditures. In other terms, the expenditure of one person is income for another person and so on.

A New Task for the State

If, however, individuals decide to consume less, this reduction in the demand for goods will result in an eventual decrease in investments and production as well as in an increase in unemployment and in inactive savings. The lack of synchronization between savings and investment constitutes — according to Keynes — the main anomaly of economic activity to the extent that it upsets the normal relationship between these two aggregates. Keynes believed it was at this point that the State should intervene to reestablish an equality between savings and investment. This means that, in the event the private saver hesitated in making new investments, the State should act to stimulate the use of savings that would otherwise remain inactive. To attain this objective, Keynes gave a new task to the State, which, through appropriate measures in the political, fiscal, social, and monetary areas, was to reestablish the economic balance and ensure full employment. Keynes expressed the view that "the State is able to calculate the marginal efficiency of capital in a long-term perspective and on the basis of the social interests of the community"; and he added that he expected to see it take "a continuously growing responsibility for the direct organization of investment."[4]

Thus, as William Beveridge, the father of the social security system in the United Kingdom, remarked, the "State will have the responsibility for a new public function." Beveridge goes still further and adds: "The State must protect its citizens from mass unemployment as energetically as it is its duty to defend its citizens from external attack or from robbery and violence."[5] And many years later, the very same message was echoed in the United States by the Humphrey-Hawkins Full Employment and Balanced Growth Act of 1978.

This Keynesian policy was applied successfully after the Second World War until the beginning of the decade of the 1970s. Countries like the United Kingdom, Australia, Canada, Sweden, the United States, and France successively adopted the ideas of Keynes on full employment policy and social welfare.[6]

In this regard it is relevant to recall the experience of the United Kingdom, which was characterized by two great new efforts — to achieve *full employment* and to ensure *social security*. In 1944 the British government adopted the Beveridge Plan on social security that had been proposed already in 1942 and whose objective was to overcome poverty and misery and to guarantee a minimum income for each person. According to the Beveridge Plan, "No citizen ready to work to the extent of his abilities would be deprived of the income indispensable to take care at all times of his essential needs and those of his family."

In 1944, also, the British government published a White Paper on employment policy that marked a step forward. For the first time, the government accepted as "one of their primary aims and responsibilities the maintenance of a high and stable level of employment after the war."

What a revolution this was in the attitudes and in the ways of thinking of the British leaders with respect to employment! Fifteen years earlier, in 1929, the Chancellor of the Exchequer had declared in the House of Commons that "in no way could the State furnish employment in a permanent way."

The reconstruction of the European countries that emerged ruined from the Second World War was made possible by their governments' development efforts and the measures taken by them to utilize fully their national resources. This brought about an improvement in the very low living levels of their populations, the creation of an "effective demand" sufficient to ensure full employment, a large increase in production, and the control of inflation at low levels. These efforts and measures were mainly inspired by, and represented a successful application of, Keynesian policies that originated in the 1930s.

No different than the very same Keynesian principles were also those which inspired the economic policies of the post-New Deal Era in the United States.

Since the beginning of the decade of the 1970s, however, we have entered a period of prolonged recession accelerated by a sharp increase in oil prices. The main characteristics of this recession are the coexistence of unemployment and inflation which, as we have already discussed, are taking on very disturbing dimensions; in fact, they constitute an assault on the economic system as great as that of the depression years of the 1930s.

CRITICISMS OF THE KEYNESIAN SYSTEM: DOES IT NEED TO BE ADAPTED OR ABANDONED?

From the beginning of the decade of the 1970s, the world economy entered a period of chronic stagflation, the main characteristics of which have been — as noted before — an unyielding inflation accompanied by persistent unemployment. This behavior of the world economy has provided an opportunity for theoreticians opposed to the Keynesian system to add, during recent years, new arguments against the full-employment policy, reinforcing some of the arguments they had made as soon as the Keynesian theory had been enunciated. We mention here in this connection two leading economists of the classical school, Friederich von Hayek and Jacques Rueff, who criticized the Keynesian theory as early as 1935-40.

Additionally, in a recent study (1976), Professor von Hayek emphasizes that: "unemployment today is the direct and inevitable result of policies of so-called full employment applied during the past twenty-five years." He adds that: "the present economic crisis at the same time seriously undermines the authority of political economy or at least marks the collapse of the Keynesian illusion which has been fashionable for a generation."[7]

For his part, Jacques Rueff, in two articles published in *Le Monde* before his death, takes up the thesis of his long disagreement with Keynes and repeats his criticisms, while referring to the facts of the present economic crisis.[8] According to Rueff, unemployment is due to the artificial maintenance of real wages at too high a level in relation to the general level of prices. For him, "the doctrine of full employment has opened the gates wide to inflation and unemployment. . . . It is about to destroy under our very eyes what remains of western civilization."

Are these criticisms of the Keynesian theory, which also emanate from many other economists and two other schools of thought, supply side economics and monetarism, justified?

No Theory is Eternal Without Adjustment

There are limits to every economic theory. Keynes himself recognized that his theory was not eternal: "I have given capitalism," he said, "thirty years of grace, of further life."

We are now at the end of this period, if we start from the end of the Second World War. This does not mean that we are at the final stage of the capitalist system. The present economic system has many possibilities of overcoming the ongoing economic crisis, but only if policies are rapidly readjusted to the evolution of socio-economic changes.

There is no doubt that if Keynes had lived longer he would have reexamined his doctrine in order to readjust it to the conditions and factors that have intervened in the meantime to alter the structures of society and of the world economy. Keynes based the application of his "General Theory" on a "given state of technology, resources and costs." Thirty years after the publication of his book, much has changed. New conditions have arisen and have overturned many of the old.

Technological progress, new conditions on the labor market, the social policy adopted toward the unemployed, the militarization of many economies, the insufficiency of productive investments, environmental and pollution problems, the close interdependence among the economies of all countries, the enlargement of the gap between the rich and the poor, polycentrism in international policies — all these factors — have brought about irrationality and contradictions in the functioning of the economic system so that it can no longer ensure full employment or sustained growth.

So the basic conditions of the Keynesian theory have been put to a severe test since the decade of the 1970s. The economic system has stopped functioning in a rational manner. When the system becomes less and less effective, production is reduced and an acceleration of inflation and unemployment appears.

The main cause of the present economic crisis is essentially, as we have said, an insufficiency of productive investment. In fact, the behavior of investments in the industrial world during recent years confirms this thesis that this insufficiency is also the reason for the endemic inflation by causing low growth in productivity.

Periods of stagnation have always been caused by a particularly low rate of capital formation. In the period of the great crisis of the 1930s, the net rate of capital formation in the United States fell to 1.4 percent of the national income (average for the period 1929-38) as contrasted with 10 percent during the period 1921-29 and 15 percent before 1914.[9]

Insufficient Effective Demand

In addition to the existence of a structural insufficiency of investments, it is a fact that a large part of those investments made are for purposes that are not productive, as is the case in the production of armaments. In fact, such military production takes away, as we have seen in Chapter 3, a large part of the national income that could otherwise be used for economic and social development; furthermore, it creates a disequilibrium between supply and demand.

When Keynes formulated his theory on the equalization between "savings and investment," he was especially thinking of productive investments in a volume sufficient for generating "creative effective demand." In particular, he envisaged investments whose result would be the increase of goods and services useful to, and needed by, the people.

Among the expenditures that may be characterized as unproductive are not only those for military purposes but also those allocated to the unemployed, even though the latter expenditures are necessary from the social point of view. These two categories of expenditures, because of their rapid expansion in recent years, have distorted the functioning of the economic system and have also thus, in part, undermined the effectiveness of Keynesian policies.

THE APPLICABILITY OF THE KEYNESIAN THEORY ON A WORLD SCALE

The factors we have just described, particularly the arms race and unemployment assistance, have transformed the industrial countries into "consumer societies." The expenditures for these two budgetary items have in fact increased consumption without a corresponding increase in the production of goods or services. Thus a disequilibrium between supply and aggregate demand, which causes inflation, has resulted.

The Need for a Creative Global Demand

The demand thus created is a simple demand, mainly for consumption, and it does not constitute a "creative demand" capable of stimulating investments and thus increasing productive capacity. Such a demand is only a "maintenance demand" of the existing productive apparatus, and causes a reduction in job opportunities, unemployment, as well as a reinforcement of inflationary pressures.

Now, the great problem today for the industrial countries is to generate a "creative demand" of maximum effectiveness; this is a basic condition required to induce investments. The entrepreneurs in a market economy hesitate to make new investments if they are not certain that the products of these investments will be sold on markets internal or external.

It is therefore necessary to find sufficient purchasing power for absorbing these additional goods produced. If such purchasing power cannot be secured within the national borders of a country, it must be sought elsewhere. The developing countries, which have a great need for equipment and services for accelerating their economic and social progress, have sufficient levels of unsatisfied aggregate demand but lack of the requisite purchasing power.

Here is the key to the problem. And it is here that the reapplication of the Keynesian theory on a world scale can bring a solution to the present economic crisis by generating sufficient levels of global creative demand.

A Broader Keynesian Theory

As explained above, it is necessary to broaden the Keynesian theory and apply its principles on an international scale. For, as we have so far seen, the Keynesian policies are no longer applicable in their pure or original form within the narrow confines of a single country in order to ensure employment.

On the contrary, we are of the opinion that by readjusting the Keynesian theory to the current global economic conditions and by adopting a new way of thinking about problems that have become worldwide in character, Keynesian policies will remain effective.

The basic elements of the Keynesian theory — that is "the equalization between savings and investment," the "marginal propensity to consume," the "stimulation of investments," the "distribution of income," the "role of the State," and other principles — must be applied not in the strict national framework but in a broader international perspective.

A NEW KEYNESIAN POLICY
FOR ANOTHER QUARTER CENTURY

A policy must be adopted that envisages the creation of an effective demand sufficient to ensure adequate employment on a world scale, in order to improve the standard of living, especially of populations with low incomes, just as Keynes recommended for the industrial countries. In other words, the same policy should be adapted toward the poor countries as the industrial states have practised toward their poor citizens. The notion of the "Welfare State" must be applied on a global scale.

In order to accomplish this objective, the role of the State must be viewed in an international rather than in a national context. This is another way of saying that economic policies must be globally addressed and globally coordinated rather than independently perceived and tailored exclusively to national targets.

It is in this context that an "equalization between savings and investments" can be attained, by stimulating effective demand through the "propensity to consume" of low-income countries. The elementary needs to be satisfied are so large that sustained effective demand can be ensured for a very long period, many decades. Thus, this sustained economic growth that occurred between 1945 and 1970 in the industrial countries could be resumed. This growth permitted industrial countries to secure the full employment of their populations during almost a quarter of a century.

In this way, a new dimension to the idea of development, more equitable and more humane, can be secured. The objective of development must not be limited only to an increase of productive capacity and the accumulation of wealth. It must take on a further meaning so that through profound transformation of economic, social, and cultural structures, especially in the poor countries, the development of the welfare of humanity, can be promoted. Development must be of benefit to all.

Keynes, the Precursor of the "New World Economic Order"

By interpreting the Keynesian theory in this global way, Keynes can be considered as the precursor of the "new world economic order," that today has been adopted as an objective by the United Nations.

Today a new post-Keynesian era is emerging. Now, in its global orientation the Keynesian theory can be reutilized and can become an even more effective instrument for solving global economic and social problems.

Our epoch should signify a new approach toward ideas and institutions. A new way of thinking must be adopted. We must liberate ourselves from the outmoded ideas of the past and understand the reality of our time as it emerges in a changing world.

This approach will permit us to establish a world plan, and through a global model, utilize the resources and satisfy the needs of humanity as a whole in order to combat misery and poverty, to elevate the standard of living as well as the cultural level of the people of all countries, and to achieve that through the working of the economic mechanism, in a stable and continuous manner.

Such a world plan for growth and development must be based on the realization of the interdependence of the economies of all countries, on international solidarity, on the fact that prosperity is indivisible, and that the rich countries cannot survive in the long run as islands in the midst of an ocean of misery.

If humanity is a community of people and development is an "international responsibility," then rich countries should extend their social and economic policies beyond their own frontiers and finance the poor nations as they domestically support the low-income sections of their populations. Such a new approach to the problem of socioeconomic development would benefit the entire world and particularly the industrial countries themselves.

Only a coherent and dynamic cooperation between North and South, based on a new strategy of growth and development and applicable on a worldwide scale, can realize a "new world economic order," thus ensuring prosperity and peace in the world. On this new strategy is based the Global Plan that we introduce in the next chapter.

NOTES

1. The bibliography about Keynes is abundant. We note some basic works: John Maynard Keynes, *The General Theory of Employment, Interest and Money* London, 1936 (French edition, Paris, Payot, 1942); Essays on John Maynard Keynes (27 contributors) Edited by Milo Keynes. Cambridge, 1975; A. Coddington, *Keynesian Economics* (London, 1983); H. G. Georgiadis, *Balance of Payments Equilibrium* Pittsburgh University Press, 1964. (A full Keynesian model is presented in this book and is subsequently integrated with a Leontief-like and money-flow models in addition to supplementing the Keynesian model with labor-supply and demand equations and a monetary subsector.); A. H. Hansen, *A Guide to Keynes* New York, 1953 (French edition, *Introduction à la pensée Keynésienne*. Paris, Dunod 1973); R. Harrod, *The Life of John Maynard Keynes* (London); S. E. Harris, *The New Economics. Keynes' Influence on Theory and Public Policy* (New York: A. Knopf, 1947); M. Herland, *Keynes* (Paris: Union Générale d'Editions, 1981); L. R. Klein, *Challenges to Keynesian Economics from the Supply Side, Rational Expectations, and Monetarism*. In forthcoming book of essays to be published by Blackwell, London; R. E. Lucas, Jr. and T. J. Sargent, "After Keynesian Macroeconomics," in *After the Phillips Curve: Persistence of High Inflation and High Unemployment* (Boston, 1978); D. Patinkin, *Anticipations of the General Theory* (London, 1982).; J. Robinson, *After Keynes* (London: Blackwell, 1973); J. L. Stein, *Monetarist, Keynesian and New Classical Economics* (London, 1982); M. Stewart, *Keynes and After* (London, 1967); A. Barrèze, *Controverses sur le système Keynésien* (Paris: Economica, 1975).

2. J. K. Galbraith, "How Keynes came to America," in *Essays on John Maynard Keynes* ed. Milton Keynes (New York: Cambridge University Press, 1975), p. 132.

3. *Les Grands Economistes*, Editions du Seuil (Paris, 1971), p. 255.

4. J. M. Keynes, *General Theory of Employment, Interest and Money*, p. 179.

5. William Beveridge, *Work for All*, p. 28.

6. See the description of the measures taken with respect to full employment and generally to social welfare policies in my book, *L'Etat et la Prospérité Sociale* (Paris, 1949), pp. 39 et seq.

7. See: *L'Année Economique et Sociale*, Edition du "Monde" (Paris, 1976). The same views were reiterated by Professor Hayak in a recent article in *The Economist*, June 11, 1983.

8. *Le Monde*, February 19 and 20, 1976. See also: Alain Barrère, *Controverses sur le système Keynésien* (Paris: Economica, 1975).

9. United Nations, *Survey of the Economic Situation in Europe in 1949* (Geneva, 1950), p. 229.

8

A GLOBAL PLAN TO REVIVE WORLD ECONOMIC GROWTH

TWO BASIC FEATURES OF THE PLAN

A world development plan should be the final objective of a policy that may be applied in several stages before being extended to all the countries in the world. We shall outline here an international development strategy that is based on Keynesian principles and is designed to satisfy the economic and financial needs of both the developing and the industrial countries.

Since an international community does not yet exist as an organic unit that could replace the State in its economic and social attributes, a transitional plan might be envisaged as a first step. This plan could provide an appropriate mechanism for the initial application of new policies on an international scale and thus lead subsequently to a more comprehensive world plan.

The purposes of this transitional plan would be to apply appropriate measures to cope with the present economic recession and to bring the world economy out of the present impasse, through the revival of sustained economic growth in both the industrial and the developing countries.

A Five-Year Grace Period
for Amortization of Old Debts

The plan would be based on two procedures interdependent and closely connected. The first procedure aims to permit the developing countries to be accorded financial facilities to overcome their untenable position of overindebtedness and thus to avoid inevitable financial crises, both for the banks and the developing countries.

As we have seen in Chapter 4, according to estimates of the International Monetary Fund (IMF), the external debt of the non-oil developing countries reached, at the end of 1982, the sum of $505 billion, with annual servicing charges amounting to $98 billion, of which $38 billion was for interest payments and $60 billion for amortization.[1]

The high cost of servicing the external debt is not due to interest but especially to the amounts paid for the rapid amortization, which represents 62 percent of the total of the servicing costs.[2] This results from the fact that the largest part of the debts are private loans made to a great extent by banks, and these loans, in turn, have an average life of 7 to 8 years (some are only 3 to 4 years). The loans made by governments have been arranged on much more favorable terms, at rather low interest and with a duration of about 30 years.

The present situation cannot last. The policy of granting new loans for paying the service of the old debts has limits. Already the lending banks are beginning to adopt restrictive policies in the granting of new loans, and they are worried about the servicing payments on existing debts. The tremendous amounts lent by the banks create very serious problems for the debtor countries. Brazil declared at the end of 1982 that it was unable to pay the service for January 1983 on its $87 billion debt. Mexico announced also that it could not meet payments for the service of its $80 billion debt. The same situation exists in such other Latin American countries as Argentina and Chile, and also in Africa and Eastern countries.

According to the International Monetary Fund, 32 countries were in arrears in 1981. Indeed, the situation in a number of these countries is untenable. Table 8.1, compiled from estimates of the Morgan Guaranty Trust Company, shows the debt and the debt service.

TABLE 8.1
Debt, Debt Service, and Ratio to Exports,
Selected Countries, 1983
(in billion of dollars)

	Total Debt at year-end 1982	Debt Service Payment for 1983
Brazil	87.0	30.8
Mexico	80.1	43.1
Argentina	43.0	18.4
S. Korea	36.0	15.7
Venezuela	28.0	19.9
Israel	26.7	15.2
Poland	26.0	7.8
Egypt	19.2	6.0
Yugoslavia	19.0	6.0
Philippines	16.6	7.0

Source: Morgan Guaranty Trust Company, Time, January 10, 1983.

The high ratio between service payment and debt, which surpasses for certain countries 50 percent of the amount of the debt, is due, as we said, to the fact that many loans are short-term credits.[3] So the conditions of financing are the main cause of the debt crisis. It is impossible for a country to utilize a credit in a productive manner when the obligations of the repayment of the capital are very short-term, say between five to eight years. Industrial countries usually receive credits for a much longer period, which permits the rational exploitation of the capital in such a way that the repayment of the interest and of the principal are facilitated.

How could these countries meet their obligations when these payments absorb more than the total value of their exports, as is seen in Table 8.1?

Objectives of the Arrangement

What can be done to avoid a crisis that will lead to a financial breakdown on a worldwide scale? In our opinion the following measures are necessary:

1. Suspend for a 5-year period the amortization of the capital of the existing debts of the non-oil developing countries; this amortization represents, as we have seen, 62 percent of the total of the service of the debts. That means that a 5-year grace period must be granted to debtors, during which interest will continue to be paid according to the prevailing interest rate of the international market on the entire amount of the debt. For this reason the banks would incur no loss.

2. The repayment of the capital of the old debts, which will be consolidated by country, will start again from the sixth year and the amortization of the consolidated old debts will be prolonged further for 15 years. During this 15-year period the consolidated debt will have a preferential annual interest rate of 5 percent.

This postponement of the amortization would be adopted under two conditions: (1) that the debtor countries would agree to utilize the economized amount by the postponement of the amortization for concrete economic projects; and (2) that the necessary imports in capital goods and services for their projects would be bought from the creditor countries.

The proposed arrangement refers only to the debts owed to banks and not to governments, where loans are already granted under more favorable conditions.

The total amount of the non-OPEC developing countries' debts reached at the end of 1982, $505 billion, as we have seen, of which $200 billion were to governments and $305 billion to banks. If we add to the amount owed to the banks the loans to the Eastern Countries,[4] the total amount exceeds $400 billion.[5] However, our proposal refers here to the non-oil developing countries, whose total debt is estimated at $305 billion for the year 1982.

The service of this debt is estimated at $73 billion, of which $28 billion is for interest and $45 billion for amortization. The total amount, which will be economized by the developing countries during the 5-year grace period, would be of the order of $225 billion.

Long-Term Loans under Favorable Conditions

The second procedure of this global plan would be the creation of an additional demand in the countries of the Third World, a demand that should be sufficient to stimulate investments in the industrial countries, as well as to revive sustained economic activity both in these countries and in the developing countries.

For the realization of this target, the industrial countries, members of the Development Assistance Committee (DAC) group, should grant to the developing countries new long-term loans on favorable conditions. The terms of this financing, which would be available for a period of only 5 years, would be as follows:

1. The volume of new loans would rise progressively from $35 to $50 billion per year, expressed in constant dollars, which represents 0.5 to 1 percent of the GNP of the industrial countries of the DAC.

2. The maturity of the loans would be for 20 years, with a 5-year grace period for the payment of capital.

3. No interest payment would be made during the first 5 years and subsequently the effective interest rate would be at 5 percent annually for each of the remaining 15 years.

4. The loans would be in the form of credits by each donor country and would be used by the recipients only for making purchases of capital goods and requisite services in the markets of the donor countries.

So, during the five years, the developing countries, according to a management system of which we shall speak later, would receive capital goods and services from the industrial countries of the order of $200 billion.

TOWARD A WORLD MARSHALL PLAN AND REPERCUSSIONS OF THE APPLICATION OF THE PLAN

The application of the proposed double financial system — on the one hand to postpone for a period of five years the repayment of the principal of the old debts and on the other to grant new long-term loans to developing countries under favorable conditions — would be in the interest of all parties and would have favorable repercussions, the most important of which are discussed below.

Developing Countries

The developing countries, which now bear a heavy burden of debt payments, would be relieved by the postponement of the amortization and be able to use the sums made available for development purposes. Their development projects would be reinforced by the granting of new long-term loans.

By the functioning of this double financing system, the developing countries will receive, during the five-year period, a total amount of $425 billion ($225 billion by the postponement of the amortization of the old debts and $200 billion by the new financing system).

This enormous amount would contribute to the acceleration of the economic and social projects of the developing countries, under the condition that the utilization of this amount would be for productive purposes only. This financing would have very positive effects on the industrial countries, as we shall see.

Banks

The lending banks, as a result of the proposed arrangement, would be able to avoid a serious crisis arising from the inability of the debtor countries to pay the service of the loans. According to U.S. bankers, about 10 percent of their total assets are at risk to foreign borrowers in trouble. As we have explained, this arrangement would incur no loss for the banks.

During the period of the first 5 years, the interest, as we said, would be paid to the total amount of the debt and during the prolongation period of 15 years the interest and the share of amortization would also be paid by the debtor countries. The only question is that the difference between the preferential interest rate of 5 percent and the prevailing market rate would have to be covered by a special "fund" of which we shall speak in the next paragraph. We must understand that such an arrangement would be the most realistic and beneficial solution for the banks. Other suggested facilities by international organizations are only provisional and ineffective arrangements that complicate the situation. For example, in what way could the proposed credit of $1.2 billion to Brazil by the Bank for International Settlements, serve to tide that country over until it could draw on a $4.8 billion 3-year credit from the International Monetary Fund when Brazil has an external debt of $87 billion and needs more than $30 billion for the service of this loan during the year 1983? Other countries of Latin America, such as Mexico, Argentina, Venezuela, and Chile are in the same situation. Even the recent (January 18, 1983) decision taken by the group of ten leading industrial countries during their Paris meeting, does not serve, in our opinion, to face up to the problem of foreign indebtedness. Indeed, this decision aims at two things: (1) to raise the overall lendable amount by IMF from $75 billion to $120 billion, and (2) to almost triple the pool of funds which they, as industrial countries, can borrow, from $6.4 billion Special Drawing Rights (SDRs) to $17 billion (or $19 billion).

Although these facilities are very important and could postpone progressively the inevitability of the financial crisis, they will not prevent it, because, as we know, the annual service of the present debts surpasses $100 billion.

The time has come to think seriously about this urgent problem and to take radical measures.

Industrial Countries

Industrial countries would be stimulated by the application of this plan to recover and to maintain a sustained economic growth, with a progressive reduction of unemployment and the expenditures surrounding unemployment insurance. Indeed, the postponement of the amortization of the old debts and the granting of new long-term loans would provoke a double demand from the developing countries for capital goods and services that would induce the entrepreneurs of the industrial countries to undertake new investments and thus provide new employment possibilities.

As discussed in Chapter 7, industrial countries need a new creative demand capable of stimulating the productive apparatus through new investments. To a large extent, nowadays, the demand in the industrial countries is, as we have seen, a simple demand for consumer products. Such a demand is a "maintenance demand" and not a "creative demand" capable of inducing large new investments and thus increasing productive capacity.

The developing countries, on the other hand, have enormous substantive needs that cannot be satisfied for lack of the requisite purchasing power. By utilizing the new loans and the savings resulting from the postponement of the repayment of the capital of their old debts for a period of five years, they would be enabled to accelerate their development and increase the purchasing power of their populations. Thus, an additional new demand would be created that would be satisfied mainly in the industrial countries.

Thus, the ultimate effect of the Global Plan would be to elevate countries into a position of economic partnership by enabling each to realize its comparative economic advantages in the world economy. This is a prerequisite for a free and expanding international trade and payments system.

International Capital Market

The application of the plan would also have favorable repercussions on the international market of capital, particularly in the formulation of the level of the interest rate.

Since 1975 interest rates have behaved with considerable fluctuation. According to the World Bank, average rates on the Euromarket rose from 8.44 percent in 1975 to 9.18 percent in 1978 and 13.68 percent in 1979. In 1980, interest rates continued to rise, reaching approximately 20 percent in 1981. At the present moment, Euromarket rates are around 10 percent. Is this behavior the outcome of present world economic conditions?

The rise in interest rates may be explained to a large extent, by the fact that the average growth rate in developed countries, which was 5.5 percent in the 1970-75 period, declined to 4.1 percent in the 1975-78 period and to a meager 1.4 percent in the 1979-82 period. The result has been a limited availability of capital during recent years. According to the International Monetary Fund, the share of international reserves to imports in the principal industrial countries fell from 23 percent in 1973 to 16 percent in 1980. The result was a decline in the capital available to the international market.

Concurrently, a massive shrinking in the surpluses of the oil-exporting countries has been observed. Following the rise in oil prices, the current accounts surplus of oil-exporting countries went up from an annual average of $26 billion in 1976-78 to $68 billion in 1979, reaching a record of $114 billion in 1980. But as a result of the decline in oil consumption, this surplus declined to $65 billion in 1981 and has reversed itself, according to IMF, to a deficit of $2.2 billion in 1982 and a deficit of $27.2 billion in 1983.

In the face of this situation, marked by a declining availability of capital, an increasing excess demand for capital is beginning to appear in the international market.[6] A rise in the deficits of developing countries alone from $39 billion in 1978 to $86 billion in 1980 and to $96 billion in 1982, contributes significantly to this excess demand. The rise in deficits is primarily due to the servicing of the existing external debts that these countries are obliged to pay every year and that escalated from $45 billion in 1978 to $107 billion in 1982.

Is Overindebtedness a Chronic Phenomenon of Our Times?

In addition to the deficits of the developing countries, two other factors have been upsetting the international capital market:

1. Industrial countries, which between 1975 and 1978 had a net surplus of $39.4 billion on their current accounts, registered during 1979-82 an aggregate deficit of $57.0 billion.

2. The Untied States' Government budget, whose deficit was restrained in the past, registered a deficit of $110 billion in 1982 and is expected to show in 1983 a deficit of $210 billion. The deficits will undoubtedly continue in the years to come. In addition, the current account deficit is estimated at $32 billion in 1983 in contrast to a cumulative surplus of $6 billion in the years 1981 and 1982 combined.

All these demands — the deficits of Third World countries, the deficits of the industrial countries, and U.S. budget deficits, as well as the capital needs of the private sector — can only contribute to a rise in interest rates.

In fact, the rising trend in interest rates is the consequence of a persistent increasing demand for capital in the international financial markets. This is where the deeper cause of the fluctuation in interest rates lies.

Thus, it may be concluded that the American policies alone are not primarily responsible for this anomaly in the rise of interest rates. Without doubt they bear some, but not the entire, responsibility. In a market limited from the viewpoint of availability of capital, the Americans seek to protect their own interests. Since their economy is a dominant economy in the world markets, they apply a monetary policy that aims, through high rates, to attract the import of capital. What other country so economically powerful would not act in the same manner?

Not only governments, but also enterprises and households are now heavily indebted. For example, the internal debt in the United States amounts to $5,000 billion,[7] and involves annual servicing in excess of $500 billion, of which the federal government's debt alone accounts for $133 billion. The same situation can be found in other industrial countries. In the Federal Republic of Germany, the public debt rose from 18 percent of the gross national product (GNP) in 1970 to 35 percent in 1980, and the servicing of this debt absorbs more than 50 percent of all new credits. In France, the foreign debt is relatively light and does not exceed 4 percent of GNP compared to 26 percent in the United Kingdom and 38 percent in Austria. However, in 1982 France has contracted more credits in order to balance its external finances and payments position.

The above data show that overindebtedness does not involve developing countries alone, nor industrial countries alone, but that it has become a serious global problem. It has also engulfed most of the socialist countries of eastern Europe as well. Their external debt rose from $37.8 billion in 1975 to $82.5 billion in 1980.

Therefore, the search for a solution to the problem of global overindebtedness, which, with the passage of time, has taken on alarming dimensions, should be given urgent priority if an economic and financial destabilization on a world scale is not to ensue. The postponement of the amortization of old debts of the developing countries amounting to some $57 billion annually for five years that we are proposing should result in some slackening of demand for new capital, and thus tend toward an appreciable decline in interest rates on the international capital market. Under these conditions, the average interest rate during the next 10 to 20 years could be about 10 percent.

But the problem of overindebtedness remains open for all countries. May it be foreseen that one day all countries will take appropriate measures to alleviate this enormous charge on governments, enterprises, and individuals?

Toward a World Marshall Plan

The proposed plan would operate as a new "Marshall Plan" enlarged on a global scale. But the application of such a new Marshall Plan presupposes settlement of the problem of the overindebtedness of the developing countries. This constitutes, in our opinion, a sine qua non condition for a "new Marshall Plan" as proposed here. Without this, no development policy can be successful. Unless such a settlement takes place, the economic aid given under present conditions would not be truly useful for the developing countries, because such aid would be immediately wiped out by the servicing of old debts.

Present economic aid by DAC countries, which amounts to approximately $30 billion a year, instead of being devoted to the actual development of the developing countries, is used, in fact, to service existing debts. This financial anomaly must end. It is on this point that our proposal differs from similar proposals put forward by others in recent years.

Only by addressing and solving this problem through the application, agreed on by both industrial and developing countries, of such a global plan, can an effective solution be provided at the same time for the recession that presently prevails in the major industrial countries.

The seeds of this plan have in general terms been developed in two of my previous books, *The Third World and the Rich Countries*, published in 1974[8] and, *For a New International Economic Policy*.[9] The ideas underlying the plan have begun to be adopted by a number of eminent statesmen. In particular, the Austrian chancellor, Mr. Bruno Kreisky, addressing a United Nations meeting organized in New Delhi in 1980, underlined the need for "a new Marshall Plan adapted to our times and to the new nature of the world economy." The same thought was also expressed by Mr. Jean-Jacques Servan-Shreiber in his book *Le Défi Mondial*. Mr. Servan-Shreiber stated that "the Marshal vision today is necessary for the entire planet for creating the proper policy for rich and poor alike."

Taking into consideration the enormous needs of Asian, Latin American, and African countries for equipment and services, and the volume of excess production and unemployment in the major industrial countries, one can only wonder why such a plan has not yet been adopted.

COST AND RESOURCES FOR THE PLAN

We shall now evaluate the cost of application of our proposal and the resources necessary to cover this cost.

External Debts and Private Creditors at the End of 1982

As we have seen in Chapter 4, the external debt of the non-oil-exporting developing countries at the end of 1982 was, according to IMF, some $505 billion, divided as shown in Table 8.2.

TABLE 8.2
External Debt of Non-Oil Exporting Developing Countries, End-Year 1982

	billions of dollars	total
By type of creditors		
Public debts		199.5
Governments	128.1	
International institutions	71.4	
Private creditors		305.7
Financial institutions	264.1	
Other private creditors	41.6	
By areas		
Africa	66.0	
Asia	121.4	
Europe	67.2	
Middle East	41.3	
Western Hemisphere	209.3	
Total outstanding debt, public and private		505.2
Service on outstanding debt in 1982		percent
Interest	40.8	38
Amortization	67.0	62
TOTAL	107.8	100

Source: IMF, *World Economic Outlook* (Washington, 1982), pp. 170, 173; IMF, *External Indebtedness of Developing Countries* (Washington, May 1981).

If we leave aside the debt of $200 billion to official creditors (governments and international institutions), as these loans are in principle granted on favorable terms and their service in 1982 would not exceed $17 billion, the private external debt of non-oil-producing developing countries, whether guaranteed or not, amounted to $305 billion.[10]

Cost of the Proposed Five-Year Grace Period for the Old Debts

As we have seen previously, with respect to the external private debt of the non-oil-exporting developing countries, which amounted to $305 billion at the end of 1982, we propose (1) a postponement of the payment of the principal for 5 years (grace period), during which period interest will be paid, and (2) the repayment of the capital, which will begin again from the sixth year, will be prolonged for 15 years at an interest rate of 5 percent.

The first condition of this arrangement does not involve any cost for the lenders because interest will be paid during the five-year grace period according to the interest rates prevailing in the international capital markets. It should be recognized that by so doing, the banks are locked in with such loans in their portfolio, thereby possibly incurring high opportunity costs. However, they avoid the inevitable position of being locked into financing the new deficits of their borrowers if existing loans were to default.

The cost of the second condition will be the difference between the proposed interest rate of 5 percent and the prevailing interest in the market. If we accept that the market interest rate, for reasons explained later, might be about 10 percent, the annual cost is estimated at $11 billion. Additional financing eliminating such cost will be provided from other sources, as explained below, thereby relieving the banks from any loss whatsoever.

Cost of the New Loans

As we have explained, our proposal consists of the granting, during a 5-year period, of new long-term loans of a volume of between $35 to $50 billion annually for a period of 20 years. During the period of grace, the debtors will be excused from all interest payments, which will commence on the sixth year at the preferential rate of 5 percent annually. Thus, a subsidy will be required to cover the volume of interest payments foregone during the 5-year period of grace and for the remaining 15 years the difference between the preferential rate of 5 percent and the prevailing rate on the international markets, which is, as mentioned above, assumed to be an average annual rate of 10 percent.

Thus, for the first 5 years, the various costs involved in the proposed new loans would be as follows:

	New Loans	Interest	Total
1st year	$30 billion	$3.0 billion x 5 years	$15 billion
2nd year	$35 billion	$3.5 billion x 4 years	$14 billion
3rd year	$40 billion	$4.0 billion x 3 years	$12 billion
4th year	$45 billion	$4.5 billion x 2 years	$ 9 billion
5th year	$50 billion	$5.0 billion x 1 year	$ 5 billion

Total amount
of new loans
for 5-year
period $200 billion

Total interest cost $55 billion

Annual interest charge $11 billion

The cost of the proposed plan for the first 5-year period would thus be $55 billion or a yearly average of $11 billion in interest.

Concerning the 15 years following the period of grace, the total outstanding debt incurred by the end of the period of grace will be $200 billion. The amount to be covered, in order to make up the difference in interest payments between the preferential and the market rates would be $8 billion annually, or a total of $120 billion for 15 years. Thus the total cost of the proposed plan is as follows:

Recapitulation of Costs
(in billions of dollars)

Annual interest cost for the first 5 years:

Old debts	zero
New debts (interest)	<u>11</u>
TOTAL	11

Annual interest cost for the next 15-year period:

Old debts	8
New debts	<u>8</u>
TOTAL	16

Sources of Funds

In order to meet the costs referred to above and to create supplementary facilities for an acceleration of the economic development of the Third World countries, an "International Development Fund" would be created. This fund would be made up of resources that now exist as well as new resources.

Public Aid

The United Nations in recently adopted resolutions has recommended that the industrial countries devote 0.7 percent of their GNP to assistance to the developing countries. This percentage has never been attained. The latest report of the Development Assistance Committee indicates that the percentage of public assistance to GNP amounted to an average of 0.35 percent or $25.5 billion in 1981 and $5 billion additional from the OPEC countries.

The additional interest cost of the proposed plan for the first 5 years would be $11 billion a year and $15 billion per year for the remaining 5 years. These required amounts could be amply covered by the amount of public assistance now being granted. Indeed, out of the $30 billion of assistance at present being given, a surplus of almost $20 billion would remain available. This surplus could cover about half of the amounts of new loans envisaged for the 5-year period.

This proposal might appear paradoxical. But it should be borne in mind that at present the public aid furnished to the developing countries does not serve to develop the economies and societies of these countries but rather to turn the wheels of a financing system that in reality only works in favor of the international capital market at the expense of the poor countries.

New Resources

Apart from public assistance, which as we have seen could cover the major part of the financing requirements of the system we propose, there are also several other possibilities for supporting an International Development Fund. We mention below some of these possible sources:

1. A special tax on the price of a barrel of oil might be instituted, particularly under conditions of surplus supplies. Considering that the total annual receipts of the oil-exporting countries in 1982 was about $210 billion, a tax of 3 percent — which would be about a dollar a barrel — could bring to the development fund an income in the order of $6 billion annually. This charge would be borne equally by the countries producing and those importing oil, except for the poorest countries.

2. A special tax might be instituted on the income derived from Euromarket deposits in the banks. These, according to the Bank for International Settlements, amounted in 1982 to $2000 billion. A charge of only 2 percent on the interest paid — about $200 billion a year, a tax paid at the source — would give to the International Development Fund an annual income of $4 billion.

3. Still another possibility would be to take a percentage of the increased value of gold that has enabled the central banks to make a profit of about $500 billion, based on an acquisition price of $35 an ounce and the purchasing price on the market, which is now around $450 an ounce. An extraordinary tax of 3 percent on the gold reserves that the central banks held prior to the suspension in 1961 of the Bretton Woods Accord — amounting to $39.4 billion, according to the IMF — could reinforce the International Development Fund by an amount in the order of $9 billion.[11]

There are therefore, as we see, several possibilities for finding resources to accelerate economic development. We will not speak here of the best possibility from a large source — the reduction in military expenditures, as proposed by the Willy Brandt Commission Report.

Recapitulation of Possible Resources

In conclusion, we observe that an enormous mass of capital could be made available, and its recycling would be beneficial to the economies of all countries in the world.

Let us recapitulate the possible resources:

	in billions of dollars (annually)
Existing	
Public assistance (0.35% of the GNP of the industrial countries)	25.5
Projected possibilities	
Tax on oil (1 dollar a barrel)	6.0
Tax on Eurobank deposits (2%)	4.0
Annual Receipts	35.5
Extraordinary tax on the added value of gold (3%)	9.0
TOTAL	44.5

Thus, in relation to the additional interest charges and new loans of $11 billion for the first five years and $16 billion for the next 15 years (see "Recapitulation of Costs" on page 160), an amount of about $40 billion could be obtained yearly to help the financing of the non-oil developing countries. This amount covers four times the resources required for the Plan.

The creation of a fund would be desirable for several additional reasons. First, it would make it possible to take certain specific measures to help the poorest countries and those most affected by the crisis. For these countries, whose debts amounted to $43 billion at the end of 1980, with an annual servicing requirement of $3.3 billion, one might envisage an annulment of a large part of their debts, as has also been proposed by the OECD. Such an annulment would improve the financial situation of these countries without any burden on the creditors.

Furthermore, with this fund, it might be possible also to create a Guarantee Fund to cover possible defaults of high-risk loans. On this point a very interesting proposal has been put forward by the former Governor of the Bank of Greece, Professor Xenophon Zolotas, and submitted to the United Nations.[12]

THE REQUISITE ADMINISTRATIVE MACHINERY FOR THE PLAN

An International Institution for the Financing of the Third World

In order that the impartial character of the financing be safeguarded, it would be desirable that an international institution administer the financing and recycling mechanisms between the industrial countries and the Third World.

This institution could be the World Bank, for it already has the administrative apparatus and broad experience in dealing with developing countries. It might have to be reorganized somewhat or could add these financing functions to its present structure.[13]

The World Bank should establish quotas for each industrial country, amounting to 0.5 percent of their GNP, for loans to the Third World countries. For 1982, the resulting amounts would have been as follows:

Quotas for Each Industrial Country
Amounting to 0.5 percent of its GNP, 1982
(in billions of dollars)

Country	GDP	Quota
United States	3,026.7	15.13
France	538.8	2.69
Fed. Rep. of Germany	656.6	3.28
Japan	1,048.3	5.24
United Kingdom	468.6	2.34
Netherlands	138.1	0.69
Canada	289.4	1.45
Sweden	98.6	0.50
Belgium	83.0	0.42
Australia	158.9	0.80
Denmark	55.9	0.28
Norway	56.4	0.28
Italy	347.7	1.74
Switzerland	95.8	0.48
Austria	66.7	0.33
Finland	48.3	0.24
New Zealand	24.3	0.12
TOTAL (OECD)	7,202.1	36.01

National Funds for Third World Financing

The government of each of the industrial countries would also establish, in its central bank, a "Fund for Financing the Third World" and place at the disposal of this fund an amount equivalent to 0.5 percent of GNP. This sum would be used to make loans to developing countries under the conditions already described.

Each developing country wishing to benefit from this financing would proceed as follows:

• The developing country would submit each financing demand to the World Bank indicating the preferred creditor country.

- Each financing demand should necessarily envisage investment in concrete development projects that would be part of the country's overall development plan.
- The World Bank, after examination of the projects presented, would transmit the relevant papers to the central bank of the -itor countries.
- Following the approval of the central bank, the developing country would get in touch with one or several enterprises of the creditor country and, according to its choice, purchase the capital goods or other products, services, etc., needed.
- Each enterprise that executes the order for the beneficiary country would be paid the countervalue of the sale by the central bank, which will in turn debit the "Fund for Financing the Third Would Countries" for the amount.
- Each credit granted to a developing country according to this procedure would be covered by the guarantee of the government of the borrowing country. At the end of the year, all national credits supplied by the country would be consolidated in a global loan on the favorable conditions described.

The proposed procedure should suffice to ensure a proper administration, taking into account the interests of all countries concerned.

COMMENTS ON THE PLAN

Earlier versions of this proposed plan were discussed with officials of the governments of some countries.

The response of the former U.S. Undersecretary of the Treasury, Mr. Fred Bergsten,* dated August 1977, to a memorandum submitted on this plan to the Secretary of the Treasury stated, in part, the following:

---

*Mr. Fred Bergsten, currently Director of the Institute for International Economics in Washington, D.C.

Your suggestion to finance imports by developing countries of additional capital equipment from the industrial countries by "recycling" funds through the IBRD and by rescheduling their debts is bold and imaginative. From our point of view, however, such drastic medicine is not necessary and may in fact be counter productive. . . .

We believe that the world economic situation is improving gradually. The major industrial countries are committed to targets for growth and stabilization which vary from country to country but which, taken as a whole, should provide a basis for sustained non-inflationary growth.

Mr. Bergsten continued with these remarks:

In the case of the U.S. specifically the most recent unemployment figures are encouraging, and the Carter Administration has requested a 30 percent increase in appropriations for economic assistance in the fiscal year 1978 — to a level of about 7.5 billion dollars — much of it to be channeled through the international development banks.

It is hardly necessary to point out that the forecasts of Mr. Bergsten did not materialize. In the United States:

- the percentage of unemployed, which was 7 percent in 1977 has risen to 10 percent in 1982, an increase of 40 percent;
- inflation rates, which were 6.5 percent in 1977 have continued to rise and reached 13.5 percent in 1980 and 10.4 percent in 1981, but declined to 4.4 percent in 1982.
- the rate of economic growth, which was 5.5 percent in 1977, declined to −1.7 percent in 1982.

The Risk of Inflation

Another possible objection is that the risk of inflation might be increased as a result of the application of the proposed plan.

On the question of inflation, Mr. Bergsten wrote:

If we forced the expansion of exports of appropriate capital equipment to the developing countries, we might find that the inflation effects of such a programme exceed the employment effects. Finally, the budgetary impact of the programme would be much larger than suggested in your memorandum.

And he adds:

This would contribute measurably to the budget deficit.

In response to these comments, we would point out that first of all, new investments will bring about an increase in the number of jobs and a reduction in unemployment, including its social costs, that is, public expenditures to maintain the unemployed. Such a productive use of labor will result in an increase in supplies of goods and services and thus lead progressively to a reduction in inflationary pressures. Thus, in the long term, the application of this plan is beneficial to combat inflation.

Regarding budgetary deficits, the undertaking we propose for public loans amounts to 0.50 percent of GNP as compared to 0.35 presently donated. In fact, the budgets of the industrial countries would bear only a slightly heavier burden for this assistance than they currently provide.

Indeed, the application of this plan would have positive effects, direct and indirect. The direct effect would be a reduction in the number of the unemployed, which would mean a reduction of public expenditures for unemployment assistance and a revival of economic activity. The resulting indirect effect will cause larger fiscal receipts. Thus, the application of the plan not only would not increase the risks of inflation and of higher budgetary deficits, but on the contrary would be a means of combating these two main contemporary problems.

Even if in the initial period some inflationary pressures were to be produced, these would be smaller than those produced by the increase in military expenditures and in unemployment insurance.

Recent Proposals by the Secretary of the Treasury, Donald Regan, and the Possible Role of the IMF

In his statement before the House Banking, Finance and Urban Affairs Committee on December 21, 1982, the Secretary of the Treasury, Mr. Donald Regan, showed a new and more realistic attitude concerning U.S. Policy vis-à-vis the developing countries and in particular with respect to the problem of their foreign debt. Certainly the overriding circumstances from the period of Secretary Simon and Bergsten have changed and the problems have become even more acute.

First of all, Mr. Regan clearly recognizes the interdependence of all economic problems and therefore remarked that "the mismanagement of these problems would have serious adverse effects on the United States economy — on its recovery and on its ability to create needed new jobs. Orderly resolution will minimize the potential risks for our citizens."

This statement is, in principle, nonequivocal. However, the strategy adopted by the Secretary of the Treasury, which is based on five key elements, does not seem to be one that could resolve the problem of the foreign debt.

The first and dominant key of the Regan proposals must be "domestic adjustment efforts by each country concerned, which will vary from country to country." These economic adjustments are, according to Mr. Regan, necessary "to restore a country's foreign borrowing capacity and the conditions for stable and steady economic growth."

Although we agree with the necessity of such adjustments — we consider in fact such adjustments as a necessary condition for the granting of facilities according to our plan — we think that this key element of any plan must be the consequence and not the cause of a generally adopted principle. Such a principle will entail the postponement of the amortization of existing loans to developing countries and the beginning of a new borrowing system under conditions more realistic and favorable to the borrowers.

Only such a policy would permit the relief of the developing countries, the disappearance of the risks to the banks, the creation of confidence in the financial community, and the beginning of a new era of economic growth. Without this interregnum no possibility of a new recovery can be envisaged. The measures suggested by Secretary Regan concerning the control of government expenditures, the elimination of large public deficits, and the inflationary money growth by debtor countries must be coincident with a new global policy aiming at accelerating their economic growth. A precondition for the above is the granting of a rest period, during which the economic hemorrhage resulting from short-term periods of debt repayment by developing countries would be effectively terminated and a new financial system begun.

Only a radical solution to the problem of foreign debt can create the necessary conditions for a sustained recovery and economic growth, because, as Mr. Regan rightly remarks, "the world economy is fundamentally poised for a sustained recovery" and most international observers "do not foresee the source of growth that will reignite investment and consumption decisions."

Concerning the possible role of the IMF in such a system, it is, as already noted, to help the developing countries to face their urgent obligations in order to avoid a deterioration of the existing, already serious situation. President Reagan's administration has taken a firm position in favor of increasing the regular lending resources of the IMF, by an amount not to exceed the existing capability by 50 percent. Treasury Secretary Regan believes that such an increase, coupled with an increase in stand-by funds "would be sufficient to carry us through the next five years to where I see the world economy going."

The objectives of the U.S. Treasury, as reflected in views expressed since the time of the Carter Administration and more clearly than ever before spelled out in the recent testimony by Secretary Regan, is to make the IMF the main, if not the only, source of lending to the developing countries beyond the loans that could be obtained from the international banking sources on commercial terms."[14] Were such policies to be put in place immediately they would aggravate rather than relieve the existing situation. It should be remembered that IMF loans are short-term and are accompanied by stringent adjustment requirements for the borrower. Such a system can possibly work well if we start from a situation of relative normalcy concerning the developing countries' debt obligations, that is, only *after* their present debt problem is accommodated.

Before agreement on such a solution is reached, having IMF facilities, with their concomitant adjustment requirements, as the only additional source of finance would be a safe, sure, and inevitable way of bringing about social unrest and political chaos to many countries of the Third World. As Henry Kissinger remarked in a recent article, "A policy of forcing developing countries to reduce their standard of living drastically over a long period is likely to weaken precisely those moderate governments that are the most likely to accept Western advice. If pushed too far, it risks provoking radicalism that will rally public opinion (and perhaps other debtors) by defying foreign creditors. This must be the opposite of the West's intent."[15]

AVOIDING A NEW FINANCIAL CRASH AND A NEW SISACHTIA

The arrangement we propose through our suggested plan constitutes a way out of the present impasse. Continuation of present policies will lead to an ever-deepening crisis. Relief measures are more than necessary in order to prevent not only the insolvency of the Third World but also the breakdown of the international economic and financial system.

Opinion is unanimous that there is a necessity for a rapid arrangement of the problem of the debt if we want to avoid an inevitable collapse of the financial and banking systems. The situation is indeed critical and one must be astonished about the apathy of the responsible policymakers. "The banking system of the Western world," declared the former British Chancellor of the Duchy of Lancaster, Lord Lever, "is now dangerously overexposed. If lending abruptly contracts, there will be an avalanche of large-scale defaults that will inflict damage on world trade and on the political stability of both borrowing and lending countries."[16] The *Economist* of London, in an article entitled "The Crash of 198.?" (October 16, 1982), said that the "banks feel the earth move under their feet," and pointed out that if the grant of new loans were suddenly to stop, "the consequent shattering of several hundred banks' shareholder's capital and reserves could give the West's over-frenetic stock markets quite an interesting following to the Black Friday morning. The odds are that then the Black Friday would be found to have been overdone, and the main consequence of the crash would be more meetings of commercial bankers and their regulators in pleasant spas, with the agenda no longer "how to reschedule a loan," but "how to redefine shareholder's capital and reserves." And the consequences will be not only economic, but also political. The debts of the developing countries pose a threat also to the international political order particularly in the developing countries.

Our proposed arrangement should satisfy all interested parties. On the one hand, debtor countries would benefit from an important additional source of finance that should permit them to obtain funds for new investments. On the other hand, creditor countries would be assured of repayment of capital loans with a reasonable servicing return. The developing countries have been able so far to meet their debt obligations only because they can continually obtain new loans for this purpose. But can this situation long continue?

Undoubtedly, there are limits to such a lending policy.[17] But it is not easy to escape from the circular chain of reasoning. If the private banks stop their financing, the bankruptcy of the developing countries would become inevitable and would endanger the existence of these banks, which are the main suppliers of credits, with adverse consequences on their depositors. As I stated at a conference of the Royal Institute of Foreign Affairs in London, in May 1980: "To maintain the present situation unchanged would lead in a short time to a financial crash greater than that of 1929, with repercussions which could undermine the foundations of the International Monetary System."

The moment has come for reflection and for taking appropriate measures before it is too late. In this connection we would refer to the precedent established by the philosopher Solon, in Athens in the fifth century B.C. Invited to act as arbitrator to resolve the problem of the overindebted Athenians, Solon introduced a law — which in Greek is called *Sisachtia* — according to which all old debts were annulled. Unless decisive and imaginative action is taken promptly, Solon's ancient law may become an inevitable necessity in today's world.

The fear of such a prospect is beginning to seriously preoccupy the International Monetary Fund and the World Bank as well as business circles. The American publication, *Fortune* magazine, wrote recently: "the poor countries' debts could shake the whole world."

The proposals we have developed represent a way, perhaps the only way, of avoiding a *Sisachtia*.

NOTES

1. According to estimates of the OECD, the total foreign debt of the non-oil developing countries amounted at the end of 1982 to $520 billion. The total debt of all developing countries, including OPEC countries, amounted at the end of 1982 to $626 billion (see OECD, *External Debt of Developing Countries*, (Paris, 1982).

2. During the period 1975-82, amortization payments represented some 62 percent of the annual servicing costs. After the interest rate decline in 1982, the proportion of the amortization is higher than 62 percent.

3. According to Morgan Guaranty Trust Company, the debt service payments for 1983 include interest payments and amortization not only for medium- and long-term, but also for short-term debts, but exclude assets abroad.

4. According to Wharton, *Centrally Planned Economy Outlook* (September 1982, p. 15), the external debt (in billions of dollars) of the Eastern countries was as follows at the end of 1982:

Poland	23.3
USSR	7.9
East Germany	11.0
Romania	9.9
Hungary	6.9
Czechoslovakia	3.0
Bulgaria	2.1
Yugoslavia	18.6
Total	82.7

5. According to statistics presented by the Secretary of the U.S. Treasury before the House Banking Committee in December 1982, the total outstanding debt of ten main debtor countries (Mexico, Brazil, Venezuela, South Korea, Argentina, Spain, Chile, Australia, Philippines, and Taiwan) to private banks was, as of June 30, 1982, $321.8 billion, of which $255.3 billion was to U.S. banks.

6. See also, Henry Kaufman, *Why Interest Rates Are So High* (New York, 1980).

7. According to *U.S. News and World Report* (January 25, 1982), the distribution of the total United States $5 trillion debt in 1981, was:

Governments (federal, state, local)	$1,170 billion
Business	$1,850 billion
Private individuals	$1,930 billion
Total	$5,000 billion

8. Praeger Publishers, New York, 1974.

9. This book was first published in Paris (PUF, 1976), with a preface by Guido Carli, was translated into English (Praeger Publishers, 1977); with a preface by Willy Brandt into German; Spanish, Portuguese, Italian, Roumanian, and Greek versions have also been published.

10. OECD estimates that the service of the public debt of $156 billion in 1981 was $10.9 billion (*Endettement extérieur*, p. 19). For the public debt of $200 billion in 1982, we estimate that the service would amount to $17 billion.

11. In a memorandum addressed in December 1969 to the president of the World Bank, Mr. Robert McNamara, I proposed that for the reasons that I then presented, and that were subsequently developed in my book *Gold in the Service of the Developing Countries* (Geneva: Nagel, 1970), a percentage of the added value of gold should be devoted to the development of the poor countries. This proposal was based on the fact that the added value of gold represented a patrimony belonging to humanity as a whole. This proposal, which at that time was characterized as "utopian," was later adopted by the IMF, which conducted successive auction sales of a part of the gold held by it and distributed the receipts to the poor countries. The amount realized by the IMF sales was $4.6 billion (IMF, *Bulletin*, May 1981, p. 15).

12. X. Zolotas, *An International Loan Insurance Scheme: A Proposal* (Athens: Bank of Greece, 1978).

13. The former President of the World Bank, Robert McNamara, has proposed the creation of a *World Central Bank* to permit the expansion of general financing, especially to poor developing countries.

14. Statement before the House Banking, Finance, and Urban Affairs Committee, December 21, 1982.

15. *Newsweek*, January 24, 1983.

16. *Time*, January 10, 1983.

17. The governors of the central banks of the member countries of the Group of Ten, plus Switzerland, met in April 1980 at the headquarters of the Bank for International Settlements in Basel and issued a communiqué in which they recommended a reinforcement of the supervision exercised with respect to international banking operations, because of the risks to which the international banking system was exposed. They emphasized in their communiqué that the solidity and stability of the banking system must be preserved and they stated it was necessary to avoid the "undesirable consequences" of continued lending.

9

TOWARD A
NEW U.S. INITIATIVE:
A GLOBAL MARSHALL PLAN

THE ORIGINAL MARSHALL PLAN

If the adoption of a global employment plan among industrial and developing countries as a whole does not appear at present to be realizable, the idea of regional plans might be considered. These could serve as models for a later adoption of a global policy.

Three regional plans could, in our opinion, be envisaged: an American plan, a European plan and an Eastern-bloc plan. We shall examine here only the American plan.

The adoption by the United States of such a plan, which might function as an enlarged Marshall Plan, would have very favorable consequences, on the one hand, the economies of the developing countries and, on the other hand, the American economy, itself in a stage of prolonged recession. Indeed this plan could serve as a powerful stimulant to revive economic activity.

Origins and Effects

When, on June 5, 1947, General George Marshall launched his famous plan from the platform of Harvard University, Europe was cut into two parts and was experiencing an economic, social, and political crisis. The assistance that the Marshall Plan brought helped in the fight against hunger and misery and contributed to the reconstruction of the European economy. The European countries were in fact able to benefit from this large-scale aid and to obtain spectacular results with respect to their economic and social progress.

The sum furnished to Europe from 1948 to 1952 was 80 percent in the form of gifts and 15 percent in the form of loans, with an interest rate of 2.5 percent repayable over a long period. But the Marshall Plan was also a powerful stimulant for the American economy. It had favorable effects on unemployment, on production, and particularly on the growth rate. Unemployment, which was 5.9 percent in 1949 fell to 2.9 percent in 1953. Productivity, which declined by 1.9 percent in 1949, increased by 9.1 percent in 1950 and continued to increase yearly and further increased by 4.3 percent in 1953. During the same years, capacity utilization in manufacturing increased from 74.2 percent in 1949 to 89.2 percent in 1953. The average annual growth rate of GNP, which was −2.7 percent during the period 1945 to 1949, increased to an annual average rate of 6.1 percent during the years 1950 to 1953.[1]

The Americans themselves recognized the advantage of this policy, which led to a transfer of the surplus U.S. production in a manner that benefitted the American economy. According to an American economist of that period, "the surplus corresponded to the amount of money that we have had to spend in one way or another to avoid finding our economy in a vicious circle."[2]

President Eisenhower's Foresight

At that time, the Americans well understood the importance for their economy of the need to absorb its surplus production and they elaborated plans for marketing this surplus early in the postwar period.

Thus, preparations were made for (1) economic assistance to foreign countries (through UNRRA and the Marshall Plan, the total of which reached about $94 billion or more than 10 percent of the annual federal budgets); and (2) military assistance within the NATO framework.

Thanks to this policy, the United States was able not only to avoid an economic crisis but also to enter upon the most prosperous era of their history. "It must be realized that the program of foreign aid is above all a program of aid to the United States," declared Harold Stassen, director of the Foreign Operations Administration at that time.

Some governmental leaders in the decade of the 1950s had a clear vision of the problems of the USA and sought to make arrangements that would enable the economy to evolve favorably in the long term. They envisaged programs designed to ensure an expansion of the U.S. economy. While still a candidate for the presidency, General Eisenhower declared, on October 22, 1951:

I believe that in concert with our closest allies a long-term, well-conceived program should be prepared which would direct all our economic power towards the economic rehabilitation and the trade of the free world, instead of limiting ourselves to a short-term assistance carried out through isolated actions.

The speech that took up the "Point IV" idea, launched for the first time by President Truman, was the origin of the 50-year plan that the United States began to elaborate toward the end of 1954 in order to support the underdeveloped countries of Asia. Sending his report on the activities of the U.S. administration's activities with respect to foreign aid (FOA) to the U.S. Congress in March 1955, President Eisenhower drew attention to the need — after the reduction of military assistance — for economic assistance to the underdeveloped countries of Asia, Africa, and Latin America, countries that he said "were the main sources of essential raw materials and minerals and where there were several vitally important military bases."

In fact, if the application of a program of assistance to the less-developed countries had been accompanied by an economic policy aimed at the evolution of a domestic Point IV program to ensure full employment, the U.S. economy would have sustained its growth as long as that program was carried out.[3]

What a change since that time!

Eisenhower's broad vision of a long-term plan lasting for up to 50 years, that would have given the United States the opportunity to become the great benefactor of the poor countries and of the poor in the United States themselves, was abandoned by his successors. The Korean War and then the Vietnam War turned the productive machine of that great country toward military expenditures at the sacrifice of foreign economic aid and of internal social expenditures.[4] In 1949, at the beginning of the Marshall Plan, public aid was 2.7 percent of the GNP and fell to only 0.3 percent in 1982. Since 1974, the American economy — like that of other industrial countries — has fallen into a prolonged recession.

CURRENT U.S. ECONOMIC POLICIES

In antithesis to the preceding, the Reagan Administration has, from its very beginning in February 1981, taken up a more conservative position.[5] The principal characteristics of this policy have been less intervention, accompanied by a reduction in certain public expenditures; encouragement of the private sector by a reduction in taxes, in particular taxes on revenue; a large increase in defense expenditures; and the setting in motion of a restrictive monetary policy to fight inflation.

From the beginning, it was feared, if not indeed foreseen, that such contradictory policies would lead to a permanent increase in the budgetary deficit which rose from $181 billion for the 4 years, 1977-80, to an estimated $565 billion for the period 1981-84.[6] These deficits come at the end of an era characterized by the following situations in the U.S. economy:

- There was a slowing down in economic growth from a yearly average of 4 percent for the preceding three decades, to only 2.8 percent for the period 1974-79 and to less than 1 percent for the period 1980-82.
- The unemployment rate, which averaged 4.8 percent during the 1960s and 6.2 percent during the 1970s, has been steadily increasing, and exceeded the 10 percent mark during 1982.
- Productivity, which was increasing by an average annual rate of 2.2 percent, declined during the 1970s to an annual average of 0.9 percent and became negative during 1980-81 to an average of −0.7 percent.

• The inflation rate (as measured by the GNP deflator increased from a yearly average of 2.5 percent in the 1960s to 6.5 percent in the 1970s and to an average of 9.5 percent during 1980-81, while during the same two years the consumer price index registered an average annual increase of 11.9 percent, and is expected to decline further to 3 percent in 1983.

• Gross fixed investment expenditures, which during the 1970s averaged yearly growth of 2.9 percent, declined to an average of −3.4 percent during 1980-81, and by −5 percent in 1982, while the Treasury bill rate increased from an average of 4.0 percent in the 1960s to an average of 6.3 percent in the 1970s and accelerated to 11.4 percent in 1980-81, but decreased to 8 percent during 1982.

The Defense Budget:
A Destabilizing Factor?

The picture that emerges from the above statistics is one of a steady decline from what some writers called the "golden age" of the 1960s to the spartan years of the 1970s and to what appears so far to be the dismal realities of the 1980s, even though so far in the new decade energy has not been a destabilizing force. But a serious destabilizing force may emanate from the defense budget, should, as forecast, the annual rate of increase in military expenditures exceed the annual rate of growth in national product. During 1975 to 1981, the average annual growth in military expenditures was in real terms 2 percent, from $85.6 billion to $159.8 billion, (accompanied by an average yearly growth in GNP of 2.8 percent) contrasted with an expected average real annual increase of 8 percent between 1982 and 1986, from $187.5 to $356.0 billion, during which the average annual increase in GNP is forecast only at about 2 percent.[7] In other words during these years, aggregate cumulative military expenditures will reach $1.6 trillion, thereby exceeding in amount the entire GNP of the United States in 1975 which was $1,549 trillion. Thus, military expenditures, which in 1982 accounted for 23.8 percent of the budget, by 1987 will have reached 35.4 percent. Were military expenditures to increase at such rate, "the planned build-up is sufficiently rapid and concentrated that it could well lead to bottlenecks in capacity, materials and labor skills" according to OECD. "If such potential bottlenecks are to be avoided efficiently, the investment repercussions could be considerable, . . . If increased defense expenditure is not to have inflationary secondary effects or crowd out private sector activity through higher interest rates, it needs to be matched by net reductions in other net expenditure."[8]

Even if considered within the framework of the Administration's optimistic projections, such an increase in military expenditures cannot be attained without creating serious economic dislocations. According to the president's Economic Report to Congress, "The Administration projects a 3.2 percent annual rate of growth in real GNP over the period 1979 through 1987 . . . and an annual increase in capital formation of 3.5 percent."[9] Such a projection is unlikely to be attainable, considering that the average annual growth between 1979 and 1982 in GNP has been only 1.05, and of capital formation −1.0 percent. Under such economic conditions the planned increase in military expenditures is bound to lead to further adverse effects on investment and employment through the monetary sector; or, in case of accommodating monetary posture, to renewed aggravation of the inflationary problem. As Murray F. Weidenbaum, the recent chairman of the Council of Economic Advisors stated, "What worries me about the defense buildup is that these crash efforts rarely increase national security. They strain resources, create bottlenecks and contribute to horrendous deficits."[10]

If the U.S. economy is to embark on such an economic course, defense expenditures that accounted for 5.6 percent of GNP in 1981 will account for 7.8 percent in 1987. In other words, with an expected average annual rate of growth in GNP of 2 percent, as stated above, and an average annual increase in military expenditures of 9 percent to 1987, defense expenditures will have accounted for more than 30 percent of the increase in GNP. Considering that in the period 1975-81, defense expenditures accounted for 4.9 percent of GNP, the magnitude of the qualitative transformation in the composition of the national product of the United States involved in such a plan of action becomes both evident and disquieting.

In short, as already amplified in Chapter 3, together with the end of rapid economic growth, we begin to discern the end of the consumer society and the consumer era, and the beginning possibly of the "arms-race" economy.

If we consider not only the defense component of the federal budget but the entire federal budget expenditures, of which defense is planned to be but a third, of the expected change in GNP between 1981 and 1986, federal government expenditures will account for over 60 percent of the growth rate. If on the other hand GNP were to grow at the more probable rate of 2 percent during this period, then total government expenditures will account for over 80 percent of the prospective change.

This situation will have, in addition to its domestic ramifications, inevitable international effects, considering the importance of the United States in the world economy.

SOME CONSEQUENCES OF U.S. DOMESTIC POLICIES

To summarize the discussion to this point, at a time when unemployment in the United States has exceeded the 10 percent mark, the President's Economic Report to Congress proposes an average annual real increase in military expenditures of 9 percent to the year 1987, thereby also increasing the share of military expenditures in the total federal budget from 22.2 percent in 1981 to 35.4 percent in 1987.

If the U.S. economy were to embark on such a defense posture, defense expenditures will have accounted for 30 percent of the entire increase in GNP, which is expected to average about 2 percent annually during this period.

But defense decisions of such a magnitude ipso facto lock the governments into playing the preponderant and domineering force in the economy without leaving much room for private initiative, while, at the same time, they render the instrument of "fiscal policy" completely impotent and ineffective. For defense expenditures have to be determined in consideration of, not independently from, the entire spectrum of government expenditures and priorities.

Let us consider the full implications of the above military strategy. If military expenditures are to account for 30 percent of the entire anticipated increase in GNP between 1981 and 1987 and if such expenditures are to reach 35.4 percent of total federal government expenditures as stated, then it follows that the entire federal budget will account for and become the source of no less than 82 percent of the total anticipated *change* in the national product. Unless, of course, the government were to cut other expenditures. But under such circumstances what is the budgetary discretion of the government cuts?

The anticipated composition of the federal unified budget in 1987 looks as follows:

	Percent
Defense	35.4
Payments for individuals	49.0
Retirement	29.7
Unemployment	2.0
Medical care	12.0
Food, nutrition, & public assistance	3.4
Other	2.0
Interest	11.9
Other	3.7

Considering that the interest obligations of the government can be reduced only within narrow limits, when interest rates fall, the only possible source of cuts (even if only in real terms) can be in pensions, in medical care, and in the very essence of services that go to the heart of social programs for the neediest groups of society.

The above discussion is from the social point of view. But from the economic point of view as well, because of what we may call the "defense locking-in effect," by allowing the defense budget to reach such proportions, the government becomes impotent as a stimulus and a regulator of economic life through the fiscal mechanism. Were this to materialize, as stated earlier, the "golden age of the 1960s," which was succeeded by the "spartan age of the 1970s," will surely be succeeded by the "arms-race era" of the 1980s, and, as already noted in Chapter 3, by the end of the "consumer society" and the establishment of the "economy of the arms race."

The economic consequences of the "defense-locking in effect," were they to operate, would have serious domestic as well as international repercussions, because if fiscal policy as an economic weapon becomes of such limited scope, monetary policy is left as the main, if indeed under the circumstances, not the only economic-policy instrument. And if monetary policy becomes "accommodating" then an inflationary spiral with ultimately stagnating effects on new investments and growth, may ensue; if, on the other hand, monetary policy were to remain in a conservative posture, then consistently high interest and the high cost of borrowing will inevitably create "crowding out" effects for the private sector, accompanied by near-stagnating economic growth.

The international repercussions of either of these two scenarios are severe. A rekindling of the inflationary process in the United States, in addition to the effects on investment and employment already mentioned, will inevitably trigger high interest rates because of its inevitable adverse consequences on the balance of payments and the international standing of the dollar. A conservative monetary posture by the United States, on the other hand, whether autonomously decided or induced by inflation, would, as it has in the past, spread to the main industrial countries and through them to the whole world. The ability of the world economy to continue absorbing such an economic situation without very damaging economic and social dislocations, may be diminishing rapidly, considering the long period under which the world economy has already been experiencing such a situation. Speaking specifically of the countries of the Third World, as was stated in an earlier chapter, an increase in the Libor rate of one point adds to the debt burden of these countries an additional $2 billion in servicing payments. Coupled with a continuation of slow economic growth and meager prospects of exports earnings, the Third World countries, under such a scenario of world economic behavior, would surely be unable to meet the repayment schedules on their existing debts.

To summarize: the budgets of the main industrial countries are already overburdened by inflexible obligations and a further increase in defense spending will render them even more inflexible; in the absence of strong economies yielding additional tax revenue through high incomes and near-full employment, borrowing by the government to accommodate additional financial requirements will lead to higher interest rates, tight credit, and worldwide stagnation; high interest rates will render the Third World countries hopelessly impotent to cope with their debts, and defaults will ensue massively.

Given the above situation, what is needed is a plan, a global plan, since the economic problems to be solved, by their very nature transcend the boundaries of any given nation and they have to be sought, as such, on an international, that is, a worldwide rather than a domestic, that is, national scale.

The United States, as the most important economy in the world, can and should pioneer and put such a system into operation. This would not only be consistent with the role the United States has played as leader of the industrial world, but also with, and a part of, the role that that country has played in leading the world out of impending global disasters. It is then in this spirit of economic realities, and defense requirements, and in the conviction that the United States does not wish to abdicate her role in shaping the course of global history that the plan presented next is called the "American Plan" or the "New Marshall Plan."

THE AIMS AND OBJECTIVES OF A NEW "MARSHALL PLAN"

We shall try now to present the general outlines of a new American "Marshall Plan," which, in our opinion, could both stimulate the activity of the U.S. economy and contribute to a more general sustained growth of the economy of the whole World.

This plan would be founded, along the same lines as the Global Plan, developed earlier, on two concepts:

Arrangement of Old Debts

The existing Third World debts to the United States would be arranged by the granting of a 5-year grace period. The conditions of this arrangement would be identical with the global plan:

• During the five-year grace period, the repayment of the principal would be postponed, but the interest would continue to be paid according to the existing market rate. In this way, the banks would incur no loss.

- The repayment of the consolidated capital of the old debts would start from the sixth year, and the amortization would be prolonged for 15 years, with a preferential interest-rate of 5 percent to be paid by the debtors. The difference between preferential and prevailing interest rates will be covered from sources as described below.

- The amounts economized by the debtor countries, as a result of this arrangement, would be utilized for development projects. The necessary imports of capital goods and services would have to be purchased from the creditor countries, as a condition of the loans.

- A U.S. institution would be created for the administration of the proposed postponement with every debtor country.

New Long-Term Loans

The second part of this new "Marshall Plan" would consist of the granting of new long-term loans to developing countries during a 5-year period, under the following terms:

- The amount of the new loans would be equal to 0.5 percent-1.0 percent of the U.S. GNP, which would mean an annual average of $30 billion during the 5-year period.

- The maturity of the new loans would be of 20 years and the amortization would begin from the sixth year.

- During the first 5 years, the loans would be interest-free. For the remaining 15 years a preferential interest rate of 5 percent would be charged.

- The loans would be in the form of credits by the United States and could be used by the recipients only for making purchases of capital goods and requisite services from the U.S. market.

Cost of and Sources of Funds for the Proposed Plan

Let us see now what would be the cost of the application of such a plan.

Old Debts

The total claims of U.S. banks including their foreign branches, is estimated at $125 billion for the end of 1982.[11] The annual service of this debt will be of the order of $35 billion, of which $23 billion will be for the amortization of the repayment of the capital and $12 billion for the interest.

The postponed amount of the amortization for a 5-year grace period would permit the developing countries to dispose a total amount of $115 billion for their economic development. A part of this economized amount, possibly a half, would be utilized, as we said, to buy capital goods needed for their economic projects.

The cost of this arrangement would be zero for the first 5 years, as the interest would be paid by the debtors. For the next 15 years the cost would be the difference between the preferential interest rate of 5 percent and the existing market, that is, it is expected to average 10 percent and could amount to $4 billion per year during the remaining 15-year period.

New Long-Term Loans

The second part of the plan, as we have said, would consist of the granting of long-term loans for a period of 20 years overall. For the first 5 years the loans would be without interest and for the next 15 years the debtor would pay a preferential interest rate of 5 percent.

The amount of the loans would be equal to 0.7 to 1 percent of the U.S. GNP, which actually is about $3,000 billion, that is, $30 billion average for the first 5 years.

The cost of this financing for the first 5 years would be the total amount of interest, which must be charged to the U.S. budget. If one accepts that the average interest rate would be about 10 percent in the market, the total cost for the 5-year period will be as shown in the tabulation on the following page. Thus the total cost of the second part of the plan for the first 5 years will be $40 billion, that is $8 billion per year.

For the remaining 15 years the cost will be the difference between the preferential rate of 5 percent and the existing market rate of 10 percent. This cost is estimated to be about $5 billion per annum.

Year	Interest on: (in billions of dollars)	Cost (in billions of dollars)
First	25	2.5
Second	53 (28 for new loans + 25 for previous years)	5.3
Third	83 (30 + 53)	8.3
Fourth	113 (30 + 83)	11.3
Fifth	143 (30 + 113)	14.3
TOTAL COST		39.2

Total Cost

If one summarizes the total cost of this plan, it will be for the first 5 years: nothing for the cost of the arrangement of old debts and $8 billion per annum for the cost of the new long-term loans; for the next 15 years: $4 billion per annum for the cost of the arrangement of old debts, and $5 billion per annum for the cost of the new long-term loans, a total of $9 billion per annum.

Sources of Funds

The problem now is to see how to cover this cost, which will be, for the first five years, $8 billion per annum, and for the fifteen years following, $9 billion per annum.

This cost could be covered by the present public assistance of U.S. to developing countries, which in 1982 amounted to $8.2 billion. The United Nations, in a recently adopted resolution, have recommended that the industrial countries allocate 0.7 percent of their GNP for assistance to the developing countries. This proportion represents for the United States an amount of $21 billion, which is more than double the amount required by the Plan. For the financing of our Plan, only 0.3 percent of the GNP of the United States is needed to cover the cost of our Plan.

As things are now, the actual public assistance of all industrial countries which amounted during 1982 to $30 billion is utilized in the end, as we have explained, for the service payments of their old debts; for the year 1982 alone this is more than $130 billion. Without a respite period, such as we propose, it is not possible to break out of this vicious circle.

Repercussions of the American Plan

The implementation of the proposed new "Marshall Plan" would have favorable repercussions on all participants, the most important of which are the following:

• The non-oil developing countries, debtors to the United States, would obtain an alleviation of their burden for a period of 5 years. The saved amount from the postponement of the amortization of the old debts — an amount of $23 billion per year — and the granting of new long-term loans — another $30 billion amount — would permit the debtor countries to initiate development projects vital to their economic and social progress. A fundamental precondition for the success of the proposed plan would be the productive utilization of the amounts granted by the creditors. For this reason the existence of concrete economic projects in every developing country will be an absolute necessity in order to avoid waste and other uneconomical utilization of the loans. A well organized procedure, as we have suggested in a previous chapter, must control every aspect of this policy.

• The American banks which, as we have seen, have loaned $125 billion to different developing countries, would be able, by the proposed 5-year grace period, to avoid a serious crisis arising from the inability of the debtor countries to pay service charges. This arrangement would not incur any loss for the banks, because interest, as we have explained, could continue to be paid at the rates prevailing in the international market. The prolongation of the amortization period for 15 years is something usual in the industrial countries and it is a reasonable period necessary for an effective and productive utilization of a loan. The rapid amortization (7 to 8 years) and even the short-term credits of 2 or 3 years, are the main cause of the present difficulties of the banking system. Only a radical policy, such as we propose, could avoid the inevitable collapse. Different facilities suggested by international organizations so far are only provisional solutions that complicate the situation. Eventually an "insurance Fund" could be created to cover some risky cases.

• The U.S. economy would be stimulated to recover and maintain a sustained economic growth resulting in the progressive reduction of unemployment and the expenditures related to unemployment insurance. Indeed, the postponement of the amortization of the old debts and the granting of new loans would provoke a double demand emanating from the developing countries in capital goods and services, which would induce the U.S. entrepreneurs to undertake new investments and create new jobs.

As we have explained in a previous chapter, the hesitation of the industrial countries to make new investment is due to the fact that their entrepreneurs are not sure that the new goods produced by the new investment would be absorbed. The mechanism that we propose gives the assurance that the new products would be demanded for a long period. The positive effects of the first "Marshall Plan" constitute a strong argument in favor of the new proposed plan. Moreover, the initiative of the United States for the application of such a plan would reinforce its international prestige and would constitute a precedent for the other industrial countries to follow.

THE NEW MARSHALL PLAN:
A NECESSITY FOR THE U.S. ECONOMY

The application of the proposed new Marshall Plan is one of the urgent measures needed to help the U.S. economy, which is "suffering the worst recession since 1937," according to the *New York Times*.[12]

Indeed, the number of objective observers who assert that the economic situation of the United States is leading to increasing budget deficits, more unemployment, inflation, and acute social disturbances, becomes larger. We limit ourselves to noting some recent opinions. The review *Business Week* wrote: "Even in a best-case scenario the government could run up cumulative deficits of almost $300 billion in the next three fiscal years if no additional actions are taken to control the budget. Less optimistic forecasters calculate the three-year deficit at $500 billion, a massive sum that they fear would drive interest rates right back up. Unless the deficit is controlled, either the Federal Reserve Fund will be forced to buy Treasury debt itself, feeding inflation, or the government's demands for funds will drive private borrowers out of the credit markets altogether."[13]

The fear of a high inflation rate is expressed also by the former chief economist to President Reagan's administration. In an interview Mr. Murray L. Weidenbaum, declared: "What worries me about the defense buildup is that these crash efforts (for the defense) rarely increase national security. They strain resources, create bottlenecks and contribute to "horrendous deficits."[14]

It is probable that the whole situation of the U.S. economy, without a change in present policies, will worsen. The main disturbance is not, as we have seen in this study, that military expenditures increase, but the fact that these expenditures increase after 1980 about three times faster than the gross national product. This is the main cause of pessimistic prospects for the future of the U.S. economy.

If we assume an annual increase of defense expenditures of 3 percent, which would be an annual rate of U.S. economic growth — under certain conditions, for the next five years a surplus of about $900 billion or $500 billion, without budget deficits, could remain — after reduction of the projected amount of $1.6 trillion for military expenditures for the period 1982-87 — at the disposal of the U.S. government.

The amount of $500 billion — an average of $100 billion for every year of the period 1982-87 — could be utilized for productive investments and other economic and social expenditures that could stimulate the recovery of the U.S. economy. Studies have shown that the infrastructure needs — bridges, ports, roads, ranging, etc. — are enormous and the rebuilding of the nation's infrastructure must be, according to an expert, "the single most expensive government challenge of the 1980s and 1990s." Only such a policy could create millions of jobs and deal with the problem of unemployment. The U.S. economy has, really, a tremendous potential for dynamism. The positive effects of the first Marshall Plan constitute a strong argument in favor of a new enlarged one.

NOTES

1. Source: *Economic Report of the President*, Appendix B. February 1982.

2. James Warburg, *Victory Without War*, p. 88.

3. The economic advisers at the White House submitted to President Eisenhower in October 1955 a program of three points aimed at assisting the regions in the USA that did not benefit as much as other regions did from the prevailing prosperity. This program may be considered as a "new domestic point four" effort.

4. The cost of the two wars (Korean War and Vietnam War) amounted to $511 billion (dollars of 1982), (Korean War $199 billion, Vietnam War $312 billion) and the cost of benefits to veterans of the two wars to $175 billion ($76.3 billion and $98.9 billion). (See *U.S. News and World Report*, October 25, 1982).

5. OECD, Economic Survey, *United States*, June 1982.

6. *U.S. News & World Report*, February 7, 1983.

7. OECD, *United States*, p. 56.

8. OECD, *United States*, p. 57.

9. *Economic Report of the President*, February 1982, p. 115.

10. *International Herald Tribune*, August 27, 1982.

11. According to a document of IMF, the total of claims of the U.S. banks in the middle of 1982 amounted to $419.2 billion of which $260 billion was to industrial countries and $111.4 billion to non-oil developing countries. To this amount, $14 billion are added for the second half of 1982. According to a statement of U.S. House of Representatives Committee on Banking (December 15, 1981), the claims (in billion dollars) of U.S. banks for the nine largest debtors were as follows as of June 30, 1982:

Mexico	25.2	South Korea	9.2	Chile	6.0
Brazil	20.5	Argentina	8.8	Philippines	5.2
Venezuela	10.7	Spain	6.7	Taiwan	4.4

12. See *International Herald Tribune*, Dec. 6, 1982. The same opinion is expressed in *Washington Post* by the well known economist Hobart Rowen. The need now is, he said, for jobs and expansion, not lower inflation (see *International Herald Tribune*, Dec. 18, 1982).

13. *Business Week*, September 6, 1982.

14. See *International Herald Tribune*, August 23, 1982.

The general conclusion of this study is that a collapse of the world economy will be inevitable should world economic policies remain on the present course. Evidence abounds on the seriousness of the ongoing worldwide stagnation; its most important characteristics, in our analysis, are listed below.

1. There is a constantly declining economic growth, insufficient to satisfy the needs of the populations of all countries and particularly of the developing countries. The average growth rate of real Gross National Product (GNP) of the industrial countries, which was 5.0 percent during the 1950s and 1960s declined to 2.8 percent for the decade 1970s and will be probably about to 1.5 to 2 percent for the 1980s, with the exception of Japan which will continue its dominant role in the Western and Asian markets.

2. There is a permanent state of unemployment acquiring progressively more alarming dimensions, with the inevitable cumulative economic, social, and political dislocations. The present number of 35 million unemployed in the industrial countries alone — with a probable increase of 2 to 3 million per year during at least the next five years — will constitute a highly destabilizing factor with serious social and political consequences.

This situation will be further aggravated by the continuing rapid progress of technology, which results, as earlier discussed, in expanded production with ever-diminishing labor inputs, thereby aggravating unemployment. It is characteristic, in this connection, that in 1982, aggregate output of all the OECD countries was greater than in 1979, while aggregate employment was less in the latter year by 15 million. Doesn't this inverse relationship mandate a profound reconsideration of social policies?

3. An overindebtedness by the non-oil developing countries, which amounted at the end of 1982 to more than $450 billion to banks alone, menaces the foundations of the international financial and banking systems. The risk to the banks is inevitable if no immediate measures, like those proposed in this study, are undertaken without further delay. To understand the gravity of the debt problem one need only recall that the seven developing countries with the highest debt to private banks, which amounted to $327 billion at the end of 1982, are required to make service payments of $150.9 billion in 1983 alone, an amount equal to 46 percent of their total debt.

Is such a situation viable and if so for how long and at what political cost? In such circumstances, the credit facilities suggested by international organizations don't constitute a solution to this urgent and alarming problem.

4. A constantly expanding militarization in all countries, including those of the Third World and particularly of the two superpowers, could lead to unthinkable consequences that menace the survival of humanity. From the moment that military expenditures increased two and four times faster than the Gross National Product — as has been the case since 1980 — the transformation of the consumer- and business-oriented economy to the arms-race economy was well under way. The first victims of such a policy are public expenditures for social and productive activities. Should the arms race between the two superpowers continue in line with policies so far in place, United States military expenditures will account for no less than 30 percent of the *entire* anticipated increase in GNP between 1981 and 1987. In the Soviet Union, defense expenditures will have reached 29 percent of consumption by 1987 and are expected to be growing at twice the annual rate of consumption. In 1982 alone, global military expenditures amounted to $700 billion, an amount exceeding one-third of the aggregate production of all developing countries, which have 75 percent of the earth's population; and by far exceeding also the total debts, private and official, of those countries. Are we aware of the problems and consequences of such a devolution?

5. There is an unyielding inflation, which, although it appears to be moderating in certain countries, will inevitably have to rise and remain high if commitment to military expenditures remains unaltered in a world that continues to experience slow growth. For slow growth restricts the tax-income yielding abilities of governments, while militarization continues to commit them to inflexible expenditures that lead to high deficits and to the impotence of the fiscal mechanism as a policy weapon. This defense locking-in effect, in conjunction with the diminution of the fiscal weapon, leaves, of necessity, monetary policy as the only regulatory economic policy. In the presence of high deficits, this, in turn means high interest rates and high inflation, as such high rates feed through the economic system.

The posture of high interest rate policy is further aggravated by unemployment insurance benefits that, in turn, aggravate public deficits and inflation further. This is so because the flow of such payments to the recipients, even though socially mandatory, is not accompanied by a counterflow in the production of goods and services.

6. The "energy-problem," which has been unanimously declared to have been a retarding economic factor during the 1970s, looms now as a Trojan horse with deceptively soothing economic signals.

The present low price of oil creates the danger that, particularly under the present state of depressed world economic conditions, governments will abandon investments in energy-saving and oil-substitute activities, with adverse effects on the economic situation in the future. For the more rapid the reduction in oil prices today, the faster the probable increase as soon as economic conditions begin to improve in the future. In addition, the present low price of oil deprives the oil-producing countries of their former ability to purchase goods and services and to provide funds for recycling to potential borrowers through the financial system.

7. Finally, there is a disturbing and ever-widening gap between the industrial and the developing countries, which causes grave economic and political impact on a planetary scale. It is unacceptable to have 700 million poor people, a number that is increasing every year, while at the same time food surpluses remain unsold in the industrial countries.

The interdependance between North and South imposes a close and constructive cooperation in facing the present recession. It must be remembered that 40 percent of the exports of the industrial countries are purchased by the developing countries and that, in turn, significant quantities of essential raw materials are imported by the former from the latter.

We must not forget also that in the year 2000, 87 percent of the active population of the entire world will be in the developing countries and only 13 percent in today's industrial countries. Thus industrial countries must clearly recognize that today's cooperation with the South is necessary for tomorrow's survival.

All these factors require an urgent change in present policies and the adoption of a new strategy for economic growth on an international scale capable of reviving and maintaining growth and of ensuring satisfactory employment levels in all countries, at least for the last quarter of the century.

The Global Plan for Employment that we propose in this study is based on Keynesian principles applicable on a world scale and is one of the most promising and feasible alternatives for handling the economic recession and reviving a sustained economic growth in the world economy.

As discussed earlier, the proposed Global Plan has two parts:

• It requires a postponement for a grace period of 5 years the amortization of the existing debts owed to the banks by the non-oil developing countries, currently of an order of $300 billion, and the prolongation of the repayment of the outstanding principal for 15 additional years. During the 5-year grace period the interests will be paid to the banks as owed, without any loss to them.

• During the same 5-year grace period the industrial countries must furnish the developing countries with 20-year loans corresponding to between 0.5 to 1.0 percent of their GNP, free of interest charges for the first 5 years, and with a privileged interest rate of 5 percent for the next 15 years.

The application of such a plan would create a sufficient aggregate demand in the developing countries to stimulate significant levels of investments and jobs in the industrial countries and in the developing countries themselves.

In other words, a new Marshall Plan will thus be created, but on a worldwide scale. The objective of the plan is to solve the problem of the overindebtedness of the developing countries and to provide at the same time a new long-term financing facility. In addition to eliminating one of the gravest debt problems in modern history, the plan will result in a fruitful cooperation between the North and South and progressively put an end to the unemployment and the poverty that are the two main evils of our times.

The success of the proposed plan will depend on the attitude of the industrial, the developing, and the oil-exporting countries. Coordinated and realistic policies inspired by international solidarity and the principle of indivisibility of global prosperity constitute essential preconditions for its success.

That the industrial countries should take the responsibility for launching a new development strategy is indisputable. And within the industrial countries the necessity for the United States to take such an initiative is also indisputable because the United States has been, and remains, the leading economic power in the world. In addition, the launching of an American Plan, along the lines developed earlier in the book, would constitute a model for other industrial countries to emulate.

On the other hand, the responsibility of the developing countries for the success of such a plan is also great. They ought to apply effective policy measures to mobilize their material and human resources and to utilize the funds granted for their economic and social development, rather than for ephemeral and often wasteful activities, as has been frequently the case. They have been entrusted with imperative duties to their people and to the world community of nations.

The oil-exporting countries, which are part of the developing world, have also a great responsibility to help their poorer counterparts in their efforts for survival. Was it not the former president of Algeria, Houari Boumedienne, who, representing OPEC before the General Assembly of the United Nations, declared that the OPEC countries would become the instrument for social justice and the promoters of the economic development of the Third World?

What a contradiction between the promise delivered then and the sad reality observed today in the single fact, for example, that the Arab, oil-exporting countries have granted $42 billion during the last three years alone to the war between Iraq and Iran! The opportunity costs of such an expenditure are both obvious and colossal.

International organizations, for their part, need to streamline and better coordinate their activities so that in place of the duplication and frequent pursuit of objectives at cross-purposes, a clearer concerted role can emerge. The International Monetary Fund and the World Bank can assume a preponderant role in administering the financial aspects of the plan; while the United Nations, abandoning its passive role, can contribute in no small measure, diagnostic, planning, and guidance services in the recipient Third World countries and in particular in the least developed countries.

The near future will show whether the industrial countries and the developing countries will fully comprehend the gravity of the present world situation, will act in a concerted manner, and will coordinate their efforts so as to bring an end to the present stagnation and to ensure world prosperity and preserve world peace.

We must not forget that the atomic age in which we live imposes — within the framework of an equilibrium of force acceptable to both superpowers — a peaceful coexistence and a constructive cooperation among all countries of the world. The continuous pursuit of a race for supremacy would lead inevitably to a catastrophe for the human race.

ANGELOS Th. ANGELOPOULOS, member of the Academy of Athens and formerly a professor at the University of Athens, is a well known economist both in Greece and internationally. For a number of years he was Director of the Economic Council of Greece. He founded and presided over the Greek Economic Planning Association and was appointed — from 1974 to 1980 — Governor of the National Bank of Greece, where he remains Honorary Governor.

Professor Angelopoulos is a member of a number of international institutes concerned with political economy, public finance, statistics, and demographic questions. He is a frequent contributor to leading journals and newspapers, and he lectures at various universities.

Among his more important publications are *Planning and Social Progress* (in French; Paris: 1953); *Will the Atom Unite the World?* (London: Bodley Head, 1957); *The Third World and the Rich Countries* (New York: Praeger, 1972); and *For a New Policy of International Development* (New York: Praeger, 1977). *Will the Atom Unite the World?* examines the economic aspects of atomic energy and has been translated into twelve languages; *The Third World and the Rich Countries* has been translated into eleven languages; *For a New Policy of International Development* has also been translated internationally with forewords by Guido Carli and Willy Brandt.